Embroidered LETTERING

Embroidered LETTERING

Techniques and Alphabets for Creating 25 Expressive Projects

Debra Valencia

DESIGN ORIGINALS
an Imprint of Fox Chapel Publishing
www.d-originals.com

Dedication

To my dear friends, who were always "angels,"
cheering me on throughout the making of this book.

Acknowledgements

My publisher's team—Tiffany Hill, Katie Ocasio, Wendy Reynolds, and photographer Mike Mihalo—has been so patient and generous with their support, and their warm reception to my project ideas and designs. I appreciate this opportunity to do what I love as my job: draw, design, teach, and sew. Thank you to my son, Westin, for his expert computer work and attention to detail on all the artwork. A big thank you to my sister, Cheyanne Valencia, for collaborating on our first sewing book together, which gave each of us the confidence to author books on our own.

ISBN 978-1-4972-0415-7

COPY PERMISSION: The written instructions, photographs, designs, patterns, and projects in this publication are intended for the personal use of the reader and may be reproduced for that purpose only. Any other use, especially commercial use, is forbidden under law without the written permission of the copyright holder. Every effort has been made to ensure that all information in this book is accurate. However, due to differing conditions, tools, and individual skills, neither the author nor publisher can be responsible for any injuries, losses, or other damages, which may result from the use of the information in this book.

INFORMATION: All images in this book have been reproduced with the knowledge and prior consent of the artists concerned and no responsibility is accepted by producer, publisher, or printer for any infringement of copyright or otherwise, arising from the contents of this publication. Every effort has been made to ensure that credits accurately comply with information supplied.

WARNING: Due to the components used in this craft, children under 8 years of age should not have access to materials or supplies without adult supervision. Under rare circumstances components of products could cause serious or fatal injury. Please read all safety warnings for the products being used. Neither New Design Originals, the product manufacturer, or the supplier is responsible.

NOTE: The use of products and trademark names is for informational purposes only, with no intention of infringement upon those trademarks.

© 2019 by Debra Valencia and New Design Originals Corporation, *www.d-originals.com*, an imprint of Fox Chapel Publishing, 800-457-9112, 903 Square Street, Mount Joy, PA 17552.

Library of Congress Cataloging-in-Publication Data

Names: Valencia, Debra, author.
Title: Embroidered lettering / Debra Valencia.
Description: Mount Joy, PA : Design Originals, [2019] | Includes index.
Identifiers: LCCN 2018050967 (print) | LCCN 2018057150 (ebook) | ISBN 9781607656654 | ISBN 9781497204157
Subjects: LCSH: Embroidery--Patterns. | Lettering--Technique. | Needlework.
Classification: LCC TT773 (ebook) | LCC TT773 .V35 2019 (print) | DDC 746.44--dc23
LC record available at https://lccn.loc.gov/2018050967

Floral graphic motifs, stitch designs, and needlework: Debra Valencia
Stitching artwork diagrams: Westin Walker
Finished project photography: Mike Mihalo

Images from *www.Shutterstock.com*: Chinnapong (textured fabric banner on cover, 6–7, 8, all project opener pages, 175); Africa Studio (background image 10–11, bottom right 32, background image 56–57); Andrius_Saz (bottom left 12); WIJI (bottom right 15); Victoria Kondysenko (top right 15); Rudenko Alla (background image 22–23); Oleksandr Lysenko (bottom 29); Miiisha (top right 34, vintage portrait 87); HomeStudio (bottom right 36); 1981 Rustic Studio kan (bottom right 42); Ekaterina43 (bottom 44); and Neo Tribbiani (bottom right 46).

Map-themed scrapbook paper on page 71 was provided by Tim Holtz's Distressables collection (0735 Traveler).

We are always looking for talented authors. To submit an idea, please send a brief inquiry to acquisitions@foxchapelpublishing.com.

Printed in China
Second printing

58

62

66

78

82

86

100

104

108

122

126

130

144

150

154

6 Contents

70

74

90

94

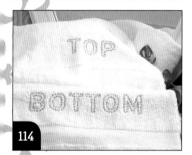

114

118

134

140

158

162

Contents

8　Introduction

10　Tools and Materials

12　Tools
14　Thread Colors
15　Fabrics
17　Design Transfer Methods
19　Finishing
20　Using Hoops for Display

22　Embroidery Stitch Guide

56　Projects

58　Hoops and Frames
90　Home Décor
118　Accessories
154　Clothing

166　Alphabets

166　Alphabet 1: Floral Monogram
167　Alphabet 2: Welcome Sign
　　　Name Drop
168　Alphabet 3: Monogram
　　　Gift Tag
169　Alphabet 4: Name Tag
170　Alphabet 5: Tennis Shoe
　　　Monogram | Left Foot
171　Alphabet 5: Tennis Shoe
　　　Monogram | Right Foot
172　Alphabet 6: Luggage Tag
173　Alphabet 7: Bonus

174　Index
175　About the Author

Introduction

I absolutely love hand embroidery! It is a lovely craft and art form. And I can multitask by stitching and watching television at the same time. It's a great way to simultaneously relax, be productive, and keep up-to-date with the news and my favorite shows.

It is so satisfying to see my designs come to life in this medium—from a loose sketch by hand, to a precise diagram on the computer, to the personality and charm of the hand-stitched design. A variety of embroidery stitches used together create such a nice combination of textures. Even for a functional name tag on a garment, I highly recommend doing stitching by hand. Machine embroidery has no heart or soul.

I typically design florals, paisleys, hand-drawn fonts, and icons in an informal Bohemian style. I am inspired by past eras, especially the 1950s, 60s, and 70s. You will likely notice a retro vibe in some of my work. Most of my designs are intended for fabric by the yard, bedding, dinnerware, and other mass-produced products by manufacturing partners. I have combined some of my favorite designs for embroidery with letters and phrases and included them in this book.

There are 25 projects in this book, unlimited possibilities using the techniques, designs, and templates provided. Embroidery may seem intimidating if you are new to needlework. I suggest practicing the stitches on a scrap of fabric before delving into a project. Once you get the hang of it, I am sure you will love it as much as I do. Once you have mastered the basics, feel free to make your own design variations by changing colors or fabrics, or by making your own phrases with the alphabets provided. Try stitching these ideas onto other projects, too—a hoop design can become a tote bag or pillow. The end results are truly precious works of art and keepsakes for years to come!

Tools and MATERIALS

Tools

Needles

I like to use needles with large eyes because they are easy and fast to thread. I suggest purchasing an assorted pack of specialty/craft needles that will include needles for embroidery, tapestry, and chenille. I used Coats & Clark® Specialty/Craft Needles, which has ten assorted sizes. There are similar assortments made by other manufacturers, including DMC and Dritz®. The smaller embroidery needles, such as a number 1, are well suited for three strands of floss. The medium embroidery needles, like numbers 2 and 3, work very well for the thicker six strands of floss and pearl cotton. The larger tapestry and chenille needles, such as number 18, work very well for ribbon.

Thimbles

I am not a thimble user. I find that they tend to get in my way. But this is entirely a matter of personal preference.

Over the years, I've heard that most people who use thimbles were taught to use them as children and it became second nature. If you have been stitching by hand all your life and enjoy using thimbles, please go ahead. If you are hurting your fingers with the needle, try out a thimble or finger protector. Experiment with one or two to see what type you prefer. There are plastic, metal, silicone, and leather thimbles and finger guards, at a variety of prices.

Embroidery Scissors

Embroidery scissors are very helpful for all needlework projects, compared to using regular sewing scissors. They are very small, with short straight or curved blades. They allow you to snip off the floss very close to the knots and fabric surface. I use Westcott® 4" (10.2cm) Sewing Titanium Bonded Curved Embroidery Scissors. I really like this style due to the super sharp blades and the way the curved shape allows it to reach into tight spaces. There are other brands making the same size scissors that may work equally well.

Antique embroidery scissors are beautiful to look at—with bird and Eiffel Tower motifs embossed in the metal. They are not as sharp as the titanium but they make wonderful decoration for your sewing table.

Hoops

I prefer wooden hoops because they are lightweight, making them easy to hold. Some crafters like plastic hoops because they tightly secure the fabric. However, this is entirely a personal preference and you should use what you like.

It is best to choose a hoop size that fits comfortably in one hand while you stitch with the other hand. It is not essential for the hoop to fully frame the embroidery design. It can be smaller and moved around the work as needed. I recommend removing the hoop from the project when it is not being worked on to avoid permanently denting the fabric with the hoop or stretching out your template. Replace the hoop each time you begin to work on the area to be stitched.

Sometimes I can find vintage embroidery hoops in thrift shops, at flea markets, and from sellers online on craft or auction sites. For a little something unusual, look for old wood hoops or plastic hoops in bright colors.

Magnifier

If you're like me and wear reading glasses, a magnifier is very useful to see the details more clearly. I find that my needlework is neater, and I can sew a lot faster with one. There are different types on the market, including magnifiers with table stands and others that can be worn like goggles. I really like the Carson® LumiCraft™ LED Lighted Hands-Free 2x Magnifier with 4x Spot Lens. The adjustable cord allows me to hang it around my neck, and it has a light that illuminates the work (or the project). It really helps to see the fabric weave better. It's not only hands-free, but it also moves along with your body, as opposed to a stationary tabletop model.

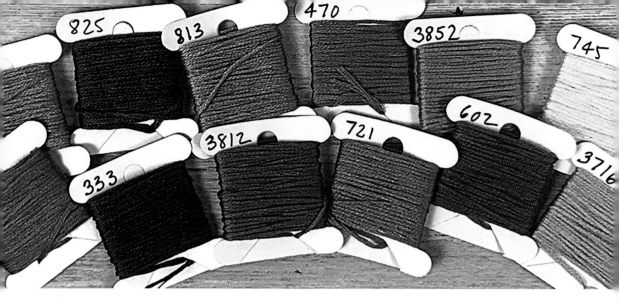

Thread Colors

All the projects in this book use DMC brand embroidery floss. There are more than 500 DMC floss colors, which create an overwhelming number of options. This brand is reliable and easy to find at my local craft stores.

Feel free to change the color choices to suit your taste or match your specific home décor and substitute any brand of thread you have access to. The DMC color numbers can be found with the color diagram provided for each project. Please note the number of strands used for each design element. I tend to use the floss in the full thickness of six strands. This is due to the larger size of the projects in this book and the appeal of the chunky look. For finer details, you may split the floss into two or three strands.

There are a lot of technical terms for colors and all of the variations of them, but I'll simplify the basics of color theory. Starting with the color wheel, there are warm colors: yellow, orange, and red; cool colors: green,

blue, and purple; and neutral colors: white, black, brown, and gray.

When choosing colors, think of them as logical ranges on the color wheel that are always winning combinations.

- Monochromatic: All shades of one color, such as light purples, basic purples, and dark purples.
- Complementary: Two colors directly across from each other on the color wheel, like orange and blue, yellow and green, or red and purple.
- Analogous: Three colors next to each other on the color wheel, such as yellow orange, yellow, and yellow green.
- Triadic: Three primary colors, which are red, yellow, and blue, or secondary colors, such as orange, green, and purple.

A color wheel and the types of color schemes are a great place to start, but ultimately you need to feel the colors and go with what you like.

Fabrics

Choosing the right fabric for hand embroidery is an essential decision; it will ensure your finished piece turns out well and supports the weight and style of stitches. It might be a good idea to try a few fabrics to see which you like best. I personally love stitching on muslin and quilt-grade cotton. Here are some tips on selecting and preparing fabric for your embroidery projects.

Thread Count

Choose fabric with the appropriate thread count and weave that will allow the needle to pull the thread easily. Fabrics with a looser weave, such as muslin, quilt cotton, linen, osnaburg, flour sack, or canvas are good. These fabrics have a lower thread count than what we might consider appropriate for bed linens or sheets. The looser the weave, the easier the needle can pass through with thread. Fabrics with a tighter weave can make it difficult, and even painful, for your fingers and hands to pull the needle and thread through.

Prewash

To avoid puckering and shrinkage, it is always a good idea to prewash and preshrink your fabric prior to stitching. This is especially important if your embroidered project will be laundered often.

Interfacing

If you are going to be adding embellishments such as beading, buttons, or thick stitching styles, you can add interfacing as a backing for your fabric. Stitching with stretchy fabrics can be a bit tricky, especially knits, and adding interfacing will make the fabric more stable.

Waste Canvas

Waste canvas is only needed when you're cross-stitching on fabrics without an

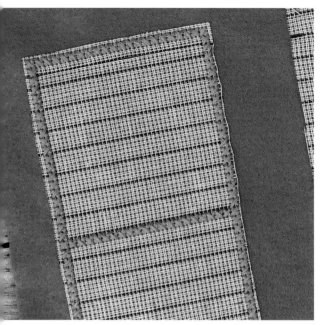
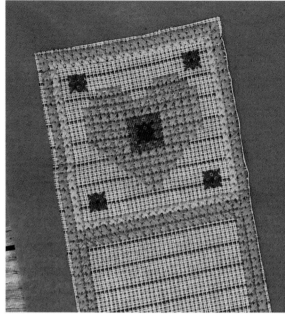

apparent even weave. It is an open-gridded, even-weave canvas with threads held together with glue and looks similar to the canvas used for needlepoint. It is available in typical counts of 8.5, 10, 14, and 18 squares per 1" (2.5cm). There is usually a blue thread woven every ten squares to assist with counting. It is called waste canvas because the material is temporary and pulled out after your stitched design is complete. Use waste canvas when you are adding cross-stitch designs on a fabric with no weave such as felt, on an uneven weave such as linen, or on finely woven fabric such as quilting cotton or silk.

To use waste canvas, mark both vertical and horizontal centerlines of the waste canvas with a disappearing-ink marker. Attach it to your project with straight pins. Starting in the center and working outward in all directions, stitch your design by counting the squares and following the cross-stitch grid diagram. When finished, remove the straight pins. Pull out the single threads of

the waste canvas with your fingers or some tweezers. Take your time so you don't distort your beautiful cross-stitching.

Ready-Made Items

Various "ready-made items" are perfect for embroidery. Try to select items made of cotton, linen, or canvas. I realize this is not always possible, and you may end up stitching on synthetic fabrics for garments or cosmetic bags. Those may be fine. Try a test stitch to make sure the needle will go through the material before committing.

Customize bedroom and bath décor with embroidered pillowcases, accent pillows, and bath towels. Dress up the kitchen and dining room with embroidered tea towels, napkins, and place mats. Personalize garments such as a shirt, cap, or canvas shoes with a monogram or name label. Make gifts by embroidering on blank tote bags, pouches, and cosmetic bags. With so many possibilities, you'll never run out of project ideas!

Design Transfer Methods

There are several methods for transferring the templates onto your fabric.

Method 1: Sulky® Sticky Fabri-Solvy™

Sulky Sticky Fabri-Solvy (*www.sulky.com*) is my favorite technique. If you have access to a photocopy machine or a scanner and a printer, I highly recommend taking this route. This is a printable self-adhesive, water-soluble stabilizer that behaves like fabric. It is available in a letter-size material that fits into any photocopy machine or laser/ink jet printer. Simply scan a design from this book and print it onto the stabilizer, or photocopy directly from the book to the stabilizer.

Mark both vertical and horizontal centerlines directly on your project with either a disappearing-ink marker or water-soluble pen or pencil. Remove the backing paper then place the stabilizer on your fabric, aligning with the centerlines. If the designs are large and utilize multiple sheets, cut along the match lines and butt the edges as you apply

them to the project fabric. Start with the pieces that align with the centerlines marked on the project. If there are any overlapping layers of stabilizer at the matching lines, trim the excess off with scissors. It is not ideal to stitch through more than one layer of the stabilizer, simply due to the extra thickness. The adhesive is very gentle and stays in place; however, I suggest securing it with straight pins or basting along the four edges of the stabilizer just to assure it doesn't move during your work on the project.

Stitch all the embroidery designs directly through the stabilizer and fabric. When it's complete, remove the basting stitches. Soak the project in water for a few minutes, and the stabilizer will dissolve instantly. While the fabric is wet, gently rub it around all the embroidery stitches with your fingers. Run it under the faucet to remove any remaining residue.

Allow your project to dry flat on a towel. To speed up drying time, firmly press some paper towels on the top to absorb any excess water. Once it's dry, you're done. It may need a slight touch-up with a warm iron. Refer to manufacturer's instructions for more details on how to use this product.

This method is highly recommended for use with felt fabric projects. The other methods do not work well with felt, as it is very opaque, and so will not work with a light table. Also, it doesn't accept transfer pens or transfer papers of any kind.

Method 2: Pen and Light Table

Make a photocopy of the template from this book onto some copier paper. Place

your paper with the template on a light table with the fabric on top. Trace the template onto the fabric with a disappearing-ink marker or a water-soluble embroidery transfer pen or pencil and center it onto a light table. If a light table is not available, you can tape your paper and fabric to a window with bright daylight coming through the back. Trace the design onto the fabric. You will stitch along the drawn lines.

When using a disappearing-ink pen, the drawn lines will . . . disappear! Depending on the brand, some will last for a few days and some will last for a few weeks. If time allows, test your disappearing-ink pen on a fabric scrap and see how long it lasts. If you plan to work quickly and finish your project in a matter of a few days, draw the entire design. If you plan to work on it a little at a time, only trace the areas you will finish within a few days. Then trace and sew each area as you continue the work.

The Dritz® Mark-B-Gone™ Marking Pen with water-soluble ink—also called a water-erasable pen—is a wonderful product. There are other brands such as the DMC® Embroidery Transfer Pen. This is my favorite option if a stabilizer is not being used. The ink is a light blue color that does not fade or disappear during the work. After completion of the project, blot any ink not covered by embroidery stitches with a damp cloth or cotton swab to remove the remaining visible pen lines on your project. The ink magically disappears with just the slightest amount of water.

One other pen option is the Pilot® FriXion® Erasable Pen. The lines can be erased with a hot blow dryer instead of submerging your finished piece in water. Be sure to test this out on sample fabric before trying it on a finished stitched piece.

Method 3: Transfer Paper

Embroidery transfer paper, dressmakers' transfer paper, and wax-free transfer paper are made by a multitude of manufacturers. Transfer paper is similar to carbon paper but made especially for fabric, with easily removable markings that do not stain your fabric. Transfer papers usually come in assorted packets, typically including white or yellow colors for transfer onto dark fabrics, and black (graphite), blue, or red colors for transferring onto white or light fabrics.

Photocopy your chosen template from this book onto paper. With the fabric on the bottom, put the transfer paper in the middle (facing down), and then place the template paper on top. Pin the design in place. Using a hard-pointed pen such as a fine ballpoint pen or pencil, trace your design by applying enough pressure to go through all layers to get a crisp line. Stitch the design along the tracing lines Since the tracing lines are usually covered by the stitching, blot any tracing lines not covered by embroidery stitches with a damp cloth or cotton swap to remove the visible lines on your project.

Finishing

Now that you have finished your masterpiece, I recommend washing it prior to ironing. It is always a good idea to wash and iron your project before adding delicate embellishments, such as beads, or ribbons.

To wash your embroidery, use running tepid water. If any hand oils have rubbed onto your finished piece, use a small amount of mild dish soap. With a drop or two of soap liquid on your palm, gently rub a circular pattern around your embroidery. Rinse thoroughly. Do not wring the water out—it can pull or distort the stitches. Lay the embroidery face up on a fresh towel or drying rack, spread flat, and let it air dry until it is just damp.

Before you iron, check for any stains or marks or remnants of transfer materials. Once you iron the embroidery, it will be difficult to remove spots. Place the piece face down on a dry bath towel. If your iron has a steam setting, make sure it is off. Use a low or medium setting and lightly press the back of the work. If there are any puckers in the stitching areas, gently stretch in both directions and press again. Do not slide the iron over the front of the embroidery, as it can snag or warp the stitches. Keep the iron constantly moving while pressing.

Now it is ready to use as-is or mounted in a display hoop or picture frame.

Using Hoops for Display

The embroidery hoop is a must-have tool for stitching, but they are also popular for framing a finished needlework piece. Try framing your next embroidery piece in a simple wooden hoop. The hoop-framing method works well, and is also easy and inexpensive. Adding a fabric back is an especially good idea for when you are making a hoop for a gift, as it looks more finished and professional.

To give your frame even more of a polished finish, try staining or painting the hoop with color or adding embellishments such as pompoms or rhinestones. You can even use a vintage embroidery hoop, as shown in a couple of projects in this book. Whether or not you decide to embellish your hoop, there are three options for finishing your embroidery hoop frame.

Glue Gun

Using a glue gun is the fastest way to finish your hoop. Position your project in the hoop with the tightening screw perfectly centered at the top. Turn your hoop facedown on a clean surface. Trim the excess fabric off with scissors, leaving about a 1" (2.5cm) selvage. With a hot glue gun, add glue to the inside rim of the hoop, applying a thin line of glue about 2" (5cm) long. Press the fabric selvage against the hoop until it sticks tightly to the surface. Add another line of glue to the next 2" or 3" (2 or 7.6cm) and press the fabric down onto the hoop. Continue section by section until the entire selvage is glued to the hoop.

Gathered Back

If you do not have a glue gun, or simply prefer to use a different method, this method only

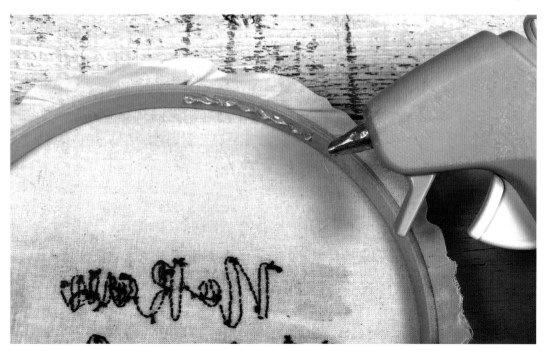

requires a sewing needle and thread. Position your project in the hoop with the tightening screw perfectly centered at top. Turn your hoop facedown on a clean surface. Trim the excess fabric off with scissors, leaving about a 1" (2.5cm) selvage. With a simple long running stitch, also called basting stitch, sew around the entire back circumference of hoop. The stitches should be about ¼" (0.6cm) from the inside edge of the hoop. When finished sewing all around, pull the thread to tightly gather the fabric. Make one or two backstitches to hold the thread tight, then tie a knot and trim off the excess thread.

Fabric-Covered Back

First, prepare a separate fabric-backing piece with quilt cotton or other matching fabric. Using the inside hoop as a template, trace a circle onto the fabric with a disappearing-ink marker. Add about a ½" (1.3cm) selvage around the entire edge. Trim the fabric with scissors along the outside line. Using a warm iron, press the selvage edge to the back with the wrong sides together. The fabric is pliable and can be bent on a curve.

Next, follow the steps for the "Gathered Back" detailed above. Then, with the hoop facedown on a clean surface, pin the fabric-backing piece (with the fabric facing right side out) to the back of hoop. With a long running stitch, sew the fabric-backing piece to the gathered back. Continue all the way around the hoop and then secure the end with a hidden knot. You may consider embellishing the edge of your hoop with ribbon, glitter, or rhinestones or various trims such as pompoms, lace, or ruffles. For hanging the hoop, simply add a short loop of ribbon, lace, or matching fabric through the tightening screw. Now your embroidery is ready for displaying, gifting, or even selling!

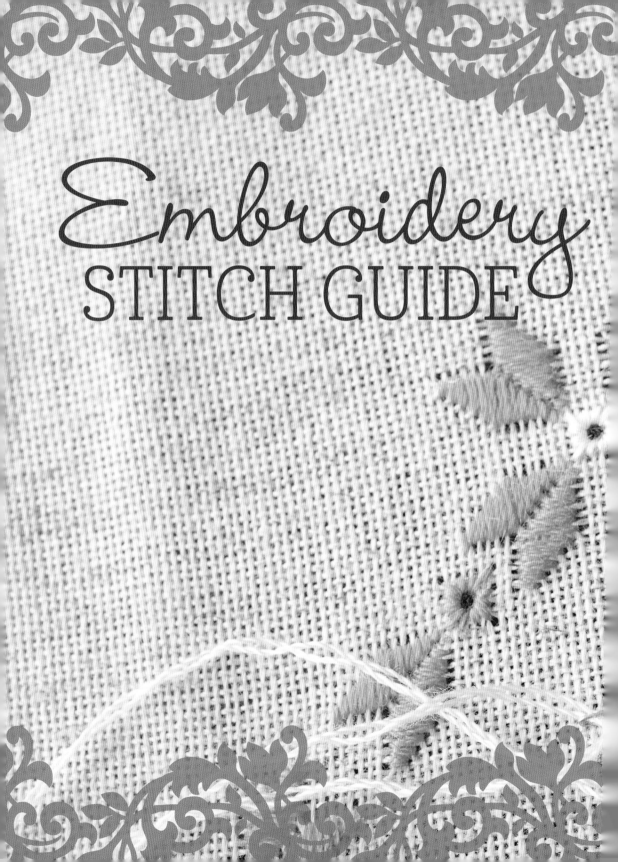

Embroidery
STITCH GUIDE

Backstitch

The backstitch is useful for fine lines and forming the outline of combination stitches.

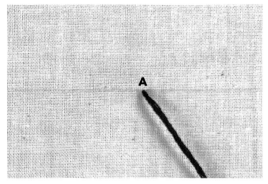

1 Draw a line on the fabric. Bring the thread to the front of the fabric at A from the end of the line.

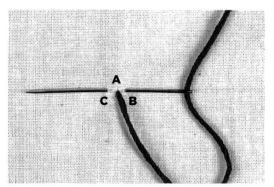

2 Take the needle to the back at B and bring the thread to the front at C. Pull the thread through to complete the first stitch.

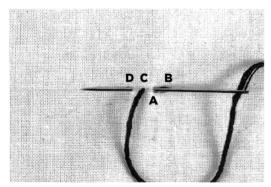

3 Take the thread to the back at point A, in exactly the same hole. Bring the thread to the front at D.

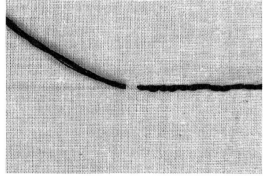

4 Continue evenly spaced stitches in the same sequence.

Blanket Stitch

The blanket stitch is very useful as an edging stitch to seam together two layers of fabric or attach an appliqué to another layer of fabric.

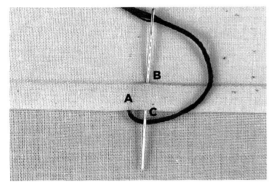

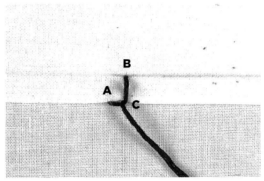

1 Draw a line parallel to the edge of the fabric. Bring the thread to the front of the fabric at A. Keep the thread under the tip of the needle. Take the needle to the back at B and bring the thread to the front at C.

2 Pull the thread through until the stitch sits snugly against the outer edge of the fabric or appliqué.

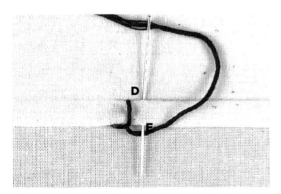

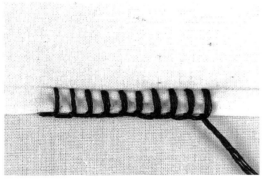

3 Take the needle to the back at D. Bring the thread to the front at E. Keep the thread under the tip of the needle.

4 Continue to work evenly spaced stitches. To end, take the needle to the back over the last loop

Colonial Knot

The colonial knot is similar, but slightly larger and higher, than the French knot (see page 34).

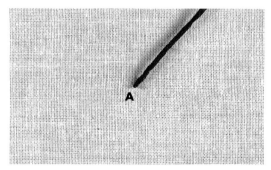

1 Bring the thread to the front of the fabric at A.

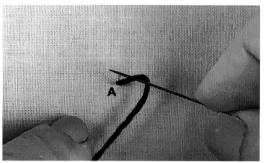

2 Hold the thread loosely to the left. With your right hand, take the needle tip over the thread. Weave the needle under the thread, close to the fabric at A.

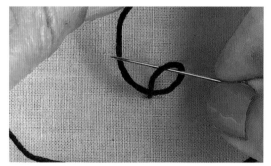

3 With your left hand, take the thread under the tip of the needle. Shorten the loop around the needle.

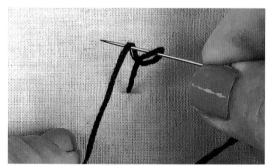

4 Then take the thread over the tip of the needle to form a figure eight.

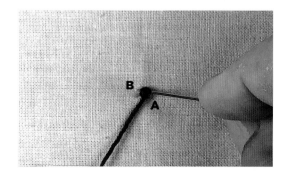

5 Pull the thread until the knot is firm around the needle. Slide the knot down the needle toward the fabric. Holding the thread tight with your left hand, take the tip of the needle close to the fabric at B, one or two fabric threads away from A. Push the needle through the knot to the back of the fabric.

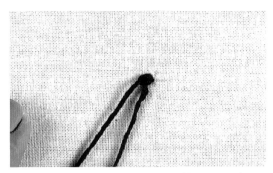

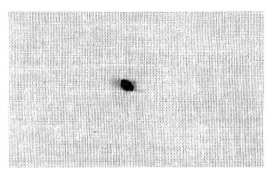

6 While holding the knot and loop on the front of the fabric with your left thumb or forefinger, continue to pull the thread all the way through with your right hand until it's tight.

7 Secure the thread on the back with a knot, or repeat these steps at the desired location for the next knot.

Couching (Trellis) Stitch

Trellis couching has a foundation of long, straight stitches anchored with small cross-stitches at the intersections.

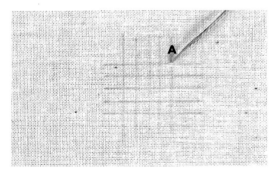

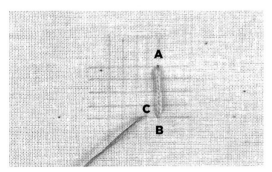

1 Draw the outline of the desired shape and mark the gridlines. Bring the thread to the front where one gridline meets the outline of the shape at A.

2 Take the thread to the back at the opposite side of the shape where the gridline meets the shape at B. Bring the thread to the front at C and pull the thread through.

continued

Couching (Trellis) Stitch continued

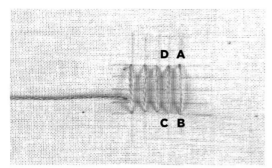

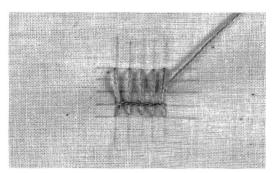

3 Take the thread to the back at the end of the same gridline. Continue until the long, straight stitches cover all of the marked gridlines. Bring the needle to the front at D on the outline at the perpendicular gridline.

4 Take the needle over the previous straight stitches and to the back at the opposite end of the gridline.

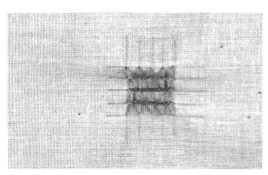

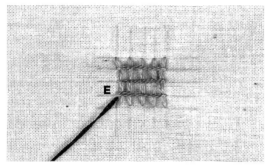

5 To complete the foundation, continue working long straight stitches across the shape until all the gridlines are covered.

6 Change the thread color. Bring the thread to the front at E, at the lower left of the intersection of the first two straight stitches. Pull through.

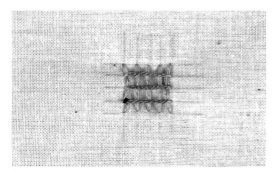

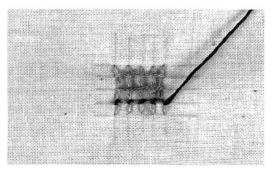

7 Form a diagonal stitch by taking the thread to the back over the foundation stitches. Pull the thread through.

8 Continue adding diagonal stitches to the end of the row. Bring the thread to the front on the lower right of the last intersection.

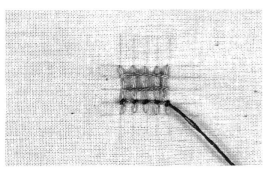

9 Form a cross-stitch by taking the thread to the back over the first diagonal stitch.

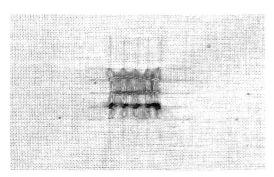

10 Continue the same sequence to complete the row.

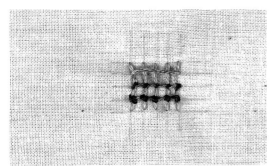

11 Follow the same sequence to complete all other rows.

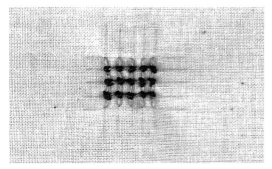

12 Completed trellis couching.

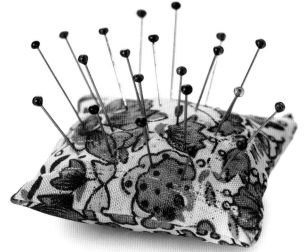

Couching (Trellis) Stitch

Cross-Stitch

The cross-stitch is made of X-shaped stitches on the fabric with an even weave or grid. The sample shown here uses waste canvas with fabric without an even weave. See page 15 for more information about waste canvas.

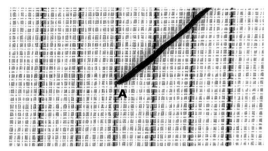

1 Bring the thread to the front at A. Pull the thread through.

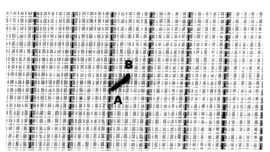

2 Counting the even numbers of squares of weave or grid, above and to the right of A, take the needle to back at B. Pull the thread through to form the first half-stitch.

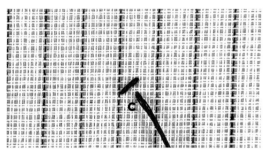

3 Bring the thread to the front at C. Take the needle to the back at D. Pull the thread through.

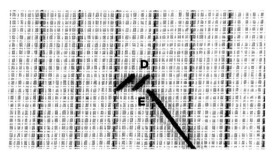

4 Bring the thread to the front at E, directly below D. Pull the thread through.

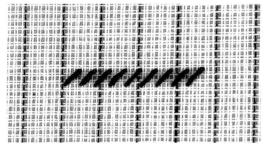

5 Continue in the same sequence until the required number of half-stitches is done.

6 Bring the thread to the front at G, directly below the end of the last stitch at F. Using the same hole in the fabric, take the needle to the back at D.

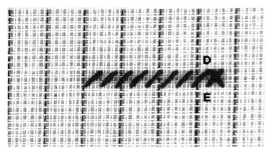

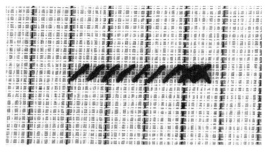

7 Pull the thread through to form the first cross-stitch. Bring the thread to the front at E through the same hole in the fabric. Take the needle to the back at D using the same hole in the fabric. Pull the thread through.

8 Continue in the same sequence to complete the row.

Fishbone Stitch

The fishbone stitch is a dense fill-in stitch with a plaited center, forming a central line.

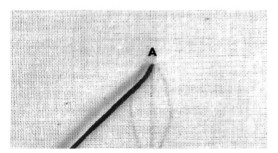

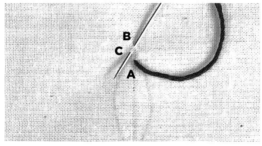

1 Draw the outline of the shape with the central line on the fabric. Bring the thread to the front at A on the centerline.

2 Take the needle to the back at B, at the end of the line, and bring the thread to the front at C. Keep the thread to the right of the needle. Pull the thread through.

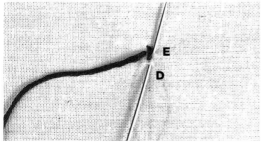

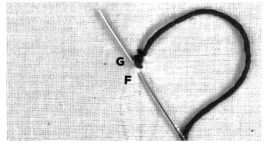

3 With the thread to the left, take the needle from D to E.

4 With the thread to the right, take the needle from F to G. Pull the thread through. *continued*

Fishbone Stitch continued

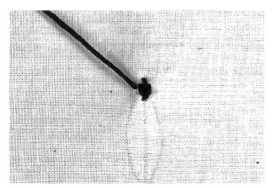

5 Pull the thread through to form the first fishbone stitch.

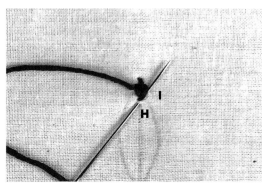

6 With the thread to the left, take the needle from H to I. Pull the thread through.

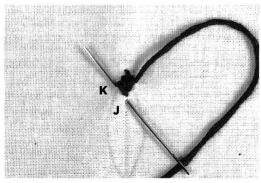

7 With the thread to the right, take the needle from J to K. Pull the thread through.

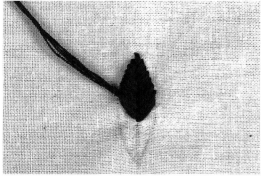

8 Continue stitching, alternating from left to right until the shape is filled.

9 Completed fishbone stitch.

Fly Stitch

The fly stitch is an open, airy fill-in stitch and works very well for leaves.

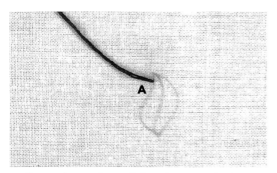

1 Draw the outline of the shape with the central line on the fabric. Bring the thread to the front at A.

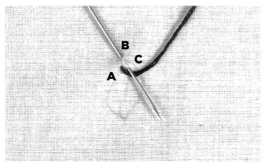

2 Take the needle to the back at B, and bring the thread to the front at C.

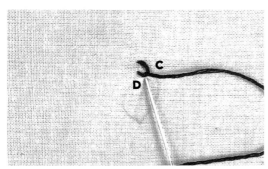

3 Take the needle to the back at D, one or two threads below C. This small stitch will anchor the loop in place.

4 Add the next fly stitch at E. Follow the same sequence until the shape is filled.

5 To finish off the leaf, bring the thread to the front at F.

6 Make one small stitch at the base of the leaf with the needle going through the fabric, right to left.

continued

Fly Stitch continued

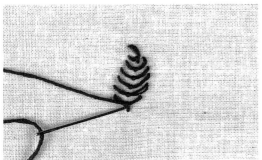

7 With the needle weaving through the thread from left to right and then back through the fabric, end with a knot.

French Knot

A French knot is a raised, round stitch made by wrapping the thread around the needle.

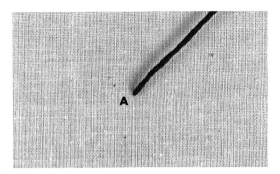

1 Bring the thread to the front at A.

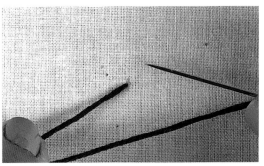

2 Hold the thread firmly with your left thumb and index finger and needle with your right hand.

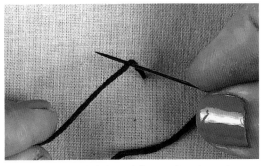

3 With your left hand, bring the thread over the needle.

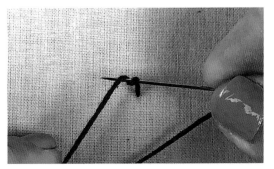

4 Wrap the thread around the needle, keeping the thread tight.

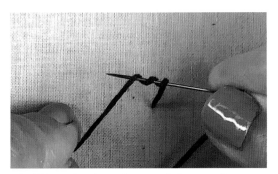

5 Wrap the thread around the needle three or four times, depending on the desired size.

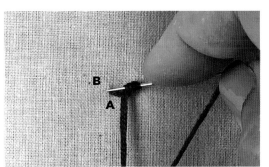

6 Pull the thread until the knot is firmly wound around the needle. Slide the knot down the needle toward the fabric. Holding the thread tight with your left hand, take the tip of the needle close to the fabric at B, one or two fabric threads away from A. Push the needle through the knot to the back of the fabric.

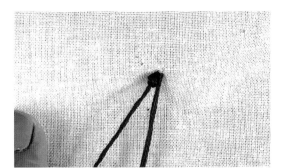

7 Holding the knot and loop on the front of the fabric with your left thumb or forefinger, continue to pull the thread all the way through with your right hand until it's tight.

8 Secure the thread on the back with a knot, or skip to the desired location for the next knot.

French Knot

Glove Stitch

This stitch looks like a zigzag and makes a very pretty border or edge stitch.

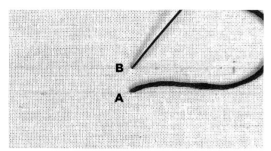

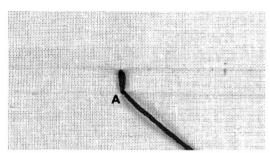

1 Draw two parallel lines on the fabric. Bring the thread to the front at A and take the needle to the back at B.

2 Pull the thread through to form a vertical straight stitch. Bring the thread to the front at A using the same hole in the fabric.

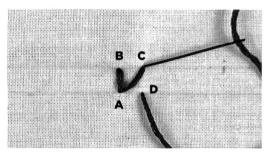

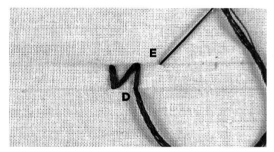

3 Take the needle to the back at C. Pull the thread through to form a diagonal straight stitch. Bring the thread to the front at D, directly below C. Take the needle to the back at C through the same hole in the fabric.

4 Pull the thread through. Bring the thread to the front at D through the same hole in the fabric. Take the needle to the back at E.

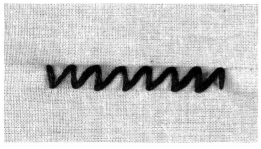

5 Continue in same sequence, ending with a vertical stitch.

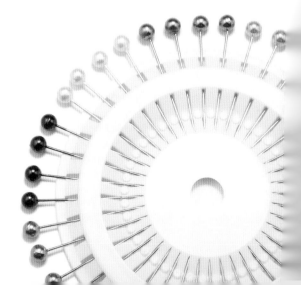

Herringbone Stitch

This stitch is often used for decorative borders.

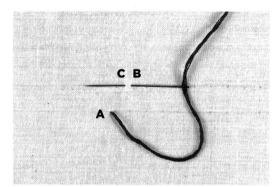

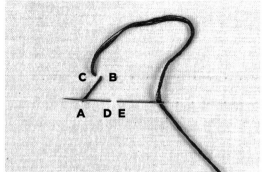

1 Draw two parallel lines on the fabric. Bring the thread to the front at A. With the thread below the needle, take the needle from the right at B to the left at C along the upper line. Make this stitch very short, approximately ¹⁄₁₆" (2mm) in length.

2 Pull the thread through. With the thread above the needle, take the needle from the right at D to the left at E. Make this stitch very short, approximately ¹⁄₁₆" (2mm) in length.

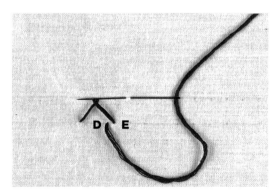

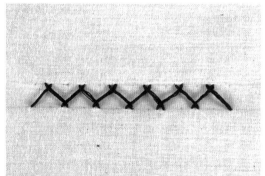

3 Pull the thread through. With the thread below the needle, continue the next stitch along the upper line.

4 Continue with evenly spaced stitches, alternating between the lower and upper lines.

Double Herringbone Stitch

This stitch is formed from overlapping rows of herringbone using two thread colors.

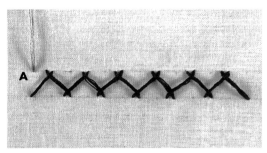

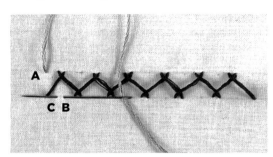

1 Make a foundation row of herringbone stitches. Change the thread color. Bring the thread to the front at A, directly above the beginning of the previous row.

2 Take the needle from the right at B to the left at C on the lower line between the stitches of the foundation row. Make this stitch very short, approximately ¹⁄₁₆" (2mm) in length.

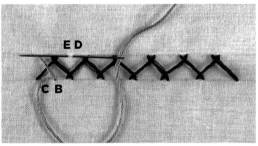

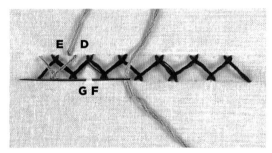

3 Pull the thread through. Take the needle from the right at D to the left at E. Make this stitch very short, approximately ¹⁄₁₆" (2mm) in length.

4 Pull the thread through. Take the needle from the right at F to the left at G on the lower line.

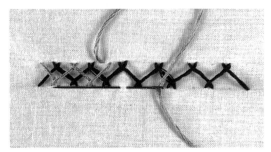

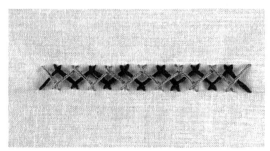

5 Pull the thread through. Take the needle from the right to the left on the upper line.

6 Continue with evenly spaced stitches over the stitches in the foundation row.

Lazy Daisy Stitch

This loop-shaped stitch can be used to create flower petals in a circle or leaves along a stem.

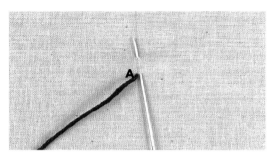

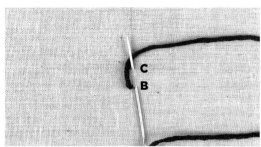

1 Knot the end of the thread. Bring the needle to the front at A.

2 Take the thread to the back at point B, inserting it as close as possible to A.

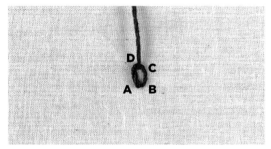

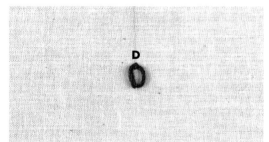

3 Bring the needle to the front at C with the thread under the needle.

4 Pull the thread through until it's snug and forms a loop. Take the thread back at D to secure the loop.

Long and Short Stitch

This dense filling stitch is especially useful for a gradual shading of colors.

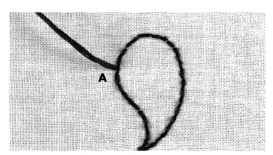

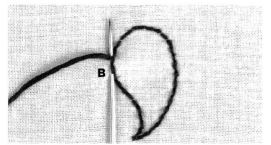

1 Draw the outline of the shape to be filled. Stitch around the shape using a backstitch to create a neat edge. Bring the thread to the front at A just outside the backstitch outline.

2 Take the needle to the back at B just outside the backstitch outline.

continued

Long and Short Stitch continued

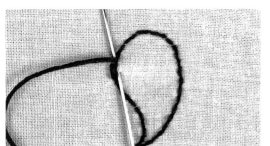

3 Add a stitch next to the first stitch. This is basically a satin stitch with varying lengths.

4 Stitch a row of straight stitches, alternating a long stitch with a short stitch.

5 Continue the row of the first thread color until it's complete. While the stitches are kept as parallel as possible to each other, they should be angled slightly to suit the shape.

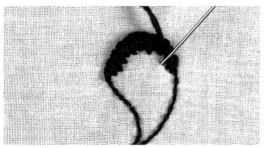

6 Add some additional rows of the first thread color as needed to fill the shape.

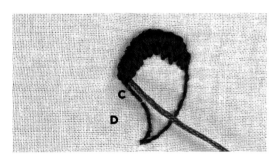

7 For the second thread color, bring the needle to the front at C, and take the thread to the back at D.

8 Continue the desired rows of stitches with the second thread color.

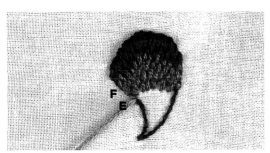

9 For the third thread color, bring the needle to the front at E, and take the thread to the back at F.

10 Continue until the entire shape is filled and the outline is completely covered.

Ribbon Rose Stitch

This beautiful ribbon rose adds dimension to your project. A ½" (12.7mm)–diameter foundation will yield a ¾" (19.1mm)–diameter ribbon rose.

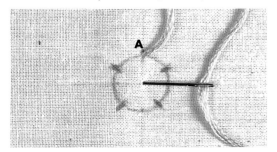

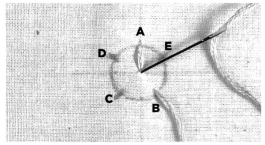

1 For the foundation, draw a circle and mark five points as shown (so it looks like a clock face). With the thread, bring the needle to the front at A. Take the thread to the back at the center.

2 Bring the needle to the front at B and take it to the back at the center. Continue the stitches for C, D, and E in the same sequence. Take the needle through the same hole in the center.

3 For the rose petals, use a tapestry or chenille needle with ribbon. Bring the ribbon to the front between the two spokes as close as possible to the center.

4 Working in a counterclockwise direction, weave the ribbon over one spoke and under the next spoke of the foundation until one round is complete. Do not go through the fabric. *continued*

Ribbon Rose Stitch

Ribbon Rose Stitch continued

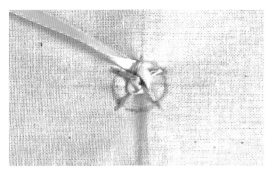

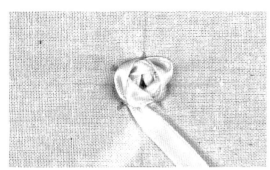

5 Weave a second round, allowing the ribbon to twist. Pull the ribbon around firmly so the threads of foundation do not show through.

6 Continue weaving, maintaining the over-and-under sequence, for two to three more rounds, until the foundation is entirely hidden.

7 After weaving the final spoke, take the needle to the back of the fabric between two spokes. Pull the ribbon through.

8 On the wrong side of the fabric, cut the ribbon and tie the two ends together.

9 The completed ribbon rose.

Rosette Stitch

Miniature roses are created quickly and easily using two thread colors.

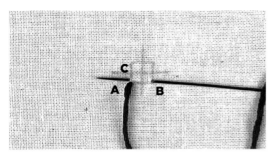

1 Draw a small square on the fabric. Bring the thread to the front at A. Take the needle to the back at B.

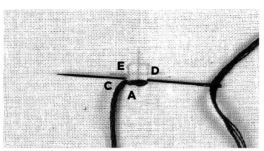

2 Bring the thread to the front at C about one to two threads above A. Take the thread to the back at D and back up at E. This is basically a satin stitch.

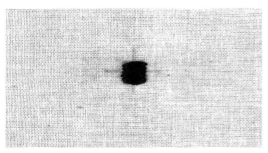

3 Make another three stitches. There are now five stitches to create a square.

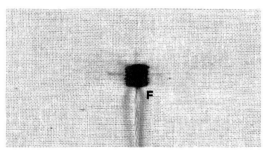

4 For the first rose petal, change to a lighter shade of thread. Bring the needle to the front at F below the stitched square.

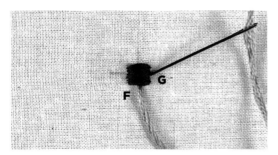

5 Take the thread to the back at G in the center of the side of the square. The thread curves slightly and overlaps the corner of the square.

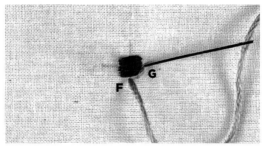

6 Bring the needle to the front just to the right of F. Take the needle to the back slightly higher than G. The stitch forms a curve just under the base of the previous stitch.

continued

Rosette Stitch continued

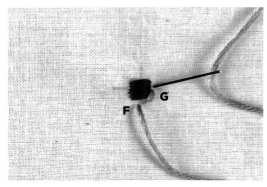

7 Bring the thread to the front just to the right of F again. Curve the thread around for the final stitch. Take the needle to the back slightly higher than G.

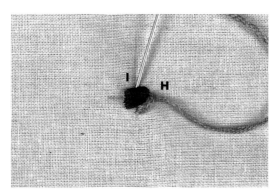

8 For the second petal, H to I, bring the needle up at H to the left of the center. Take the needle to the back at I. Add two additional stitches to the petal H/I.

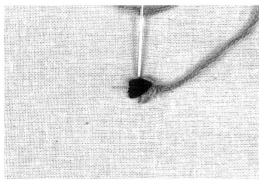

9 Follow the same steps for the remaining two petals.

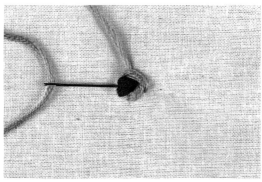

10 Completed rosette stitch.

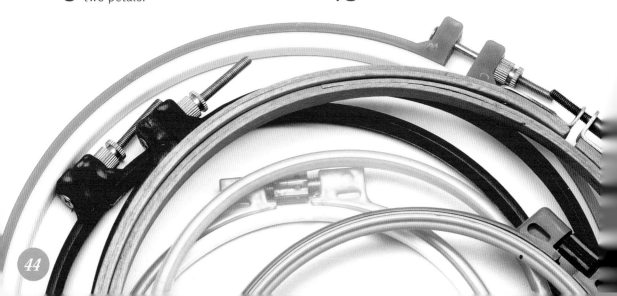

Running Stitch

The running stitch is a quick and easy-to-make line stitch. It's used to form the foundation of the combination stitches.

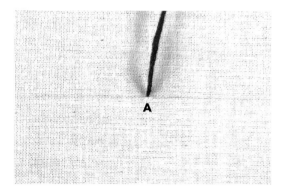

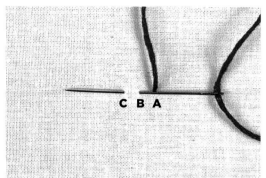

1 Draw the line on the fabric. Bring the thread to the front at A on the right-hand end of line.

2 Take the needle to the back at B and thread to the front at C. Pull the thread through.

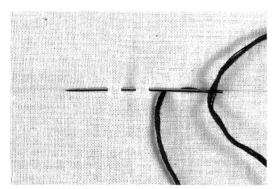

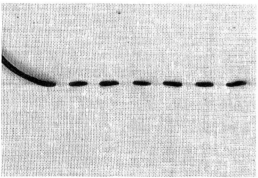

3 To save time, take several stitches that are the same length as the previous stitch at the same time.

4 Continue the same sequence to the end of the row.

Whipped Running Stitch

The whipped running stitch has a raised, corded appearance and looks best with two thread colors.

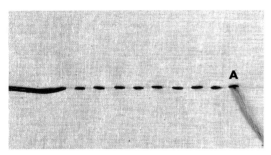

1 Draw a line on the fabric. Stitch the foundation with a running stitch.

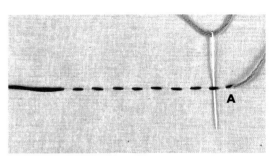

2 Change the thread color. Bring the thread to the front at A, just below the center of the first running stitch.

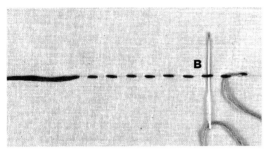

3 Take the needle from the bottom to the top at B, weaving under the second stitch. Do not go through the fabric.

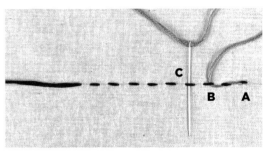

4 Pull the thread through, using loose tension. Take the needle from the top to the bottom at C, weaving under the third stitch. Do not go through the fabric.

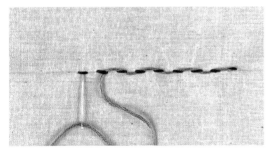

5 Pull the thread through, using loose tension. Continue in the same sequence to the end of the row.

Satin Stitch

The satin stitch is a beautiful and neat fill-in stitch.

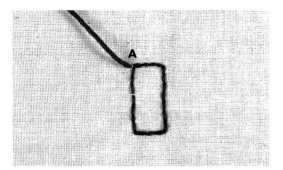

1 Draw the outline of the shape to be filled. Stitch around the shape with a backstitch to create a neat edge. Bring the thread to the front at A just outside the backstitched outline.

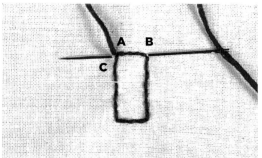

2 Take the needle to the back at B on the opposite side of the outline and bring the thread to the front at C, very close to A.

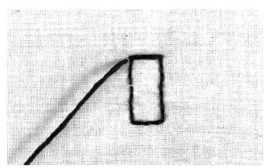

3 Pull the thread through. The first stitch should completely cover the outline.

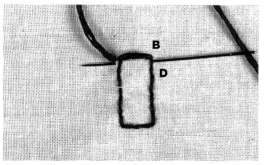

4 Take the needle to the back at D, very close to B, and lay it down parallel to the first stitch. Pull the thread through.

5 Continue stitching in the same sequence with very neat and parallel spacing.

6 Continue stitching until the shape is filled.

Seed Stitch

This stitch is a fill-in stitch and can be used to fill in letters or shapes, or scattered in a background.

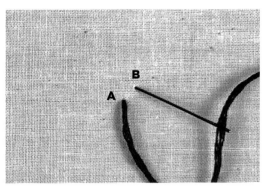

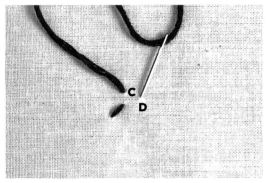

1 It is not necessary to draw any lines for this stitch unless you want to define an area to be filled. Bring the thread to the front at A. Take the needle to the back at B.

2 Bring the thread to the front at C, and take the needle to the back at D.

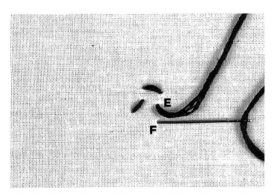

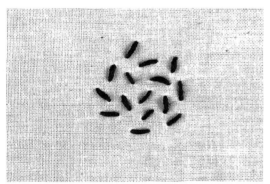

3 Pull the thread through. Take the needle to the back close at E, and bring the thread to the front at F. Vary the angle of each stitch.

4 Continue working random seed stitches in the area to be filled.

Sheaf Stitch

This stitch looks like a miniature sheaf of wheat and makes a lovely border.

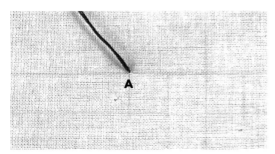

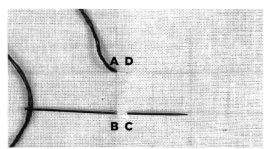

1 Draw squares on the fabric at the desired size. Bring the thread to the front at A.

2 Take the needle to the back at B to form a vertical straight stitch. Bring the thread to the front at C. Continue the same sequence at D to make the second stitch. Continue to make five vertical straight stitches to fill the square area.

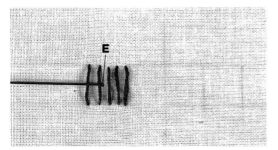

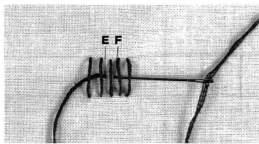

3 Bring the thread to the front at E. Take the needle from left to right, weaving under all three stitches. Do not go through the fabric.

4 Take a second stitch at F, weaving from the right to the left under the vertical stitches. Do not go through the fabric.

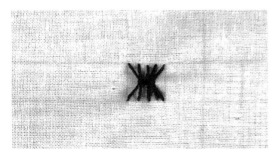

5 Pull the thread tight to make the five straight stitches tight in the center, forming the sheaf. Wrap the thread a second time, bringing the thread to the front at E, and taking the needle to the back at F.

6 Pull the thread through to complete the first stitch. For the second stitch, bring the thread to the front at G.

continued

Sheaf Stitch continued

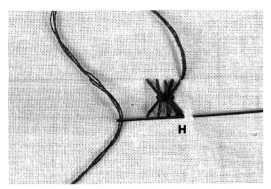

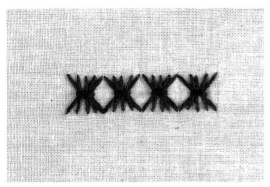

7 Take the needle back at H.

8 Continue in the same sequence for a border.

Star Stitch

The star stitch is often placed randomly on a background to add visual interest.

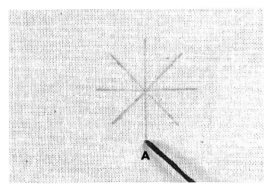

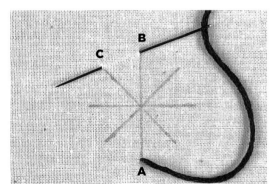

1 Draw four intersecting lines in a circle on the fabric. Bring the thread to the front at A.

2 Take the needle to the back at B, and bring the thread to the front at C.

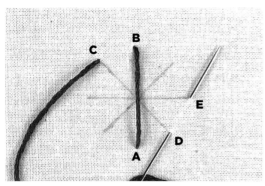

3 Pull the thread through. Take the needle to the back at D, and bring the thread to the front at E. This stitch will cross over the first stitch.

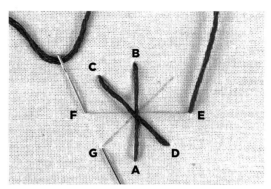

4 Pull the thread through. Take the needle to the back at F, and bring the thread to the front at G.

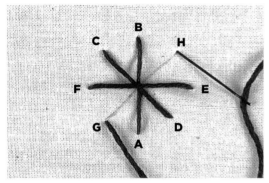

5 Pull the thread through. Take the needle to the back at H, to form the final spoke of the star.

6 Bring the needle to the front, near the center between the two spokes.

7 Take the needle over the intersection of spokes, and to back near the center.

8 Pull the thread through to anchor the spokes at the center.

Stem Stitch

This versatile stitch is used for making raised lines with a corded look.

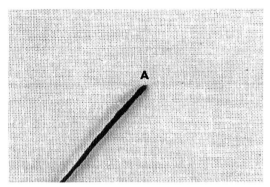

1 Draw a line on the fabric. Bring the needle to the front at A.

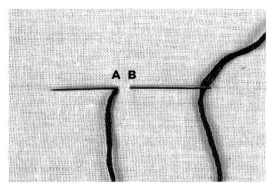

2 With the thread below the needle, take the thread to the back at B. Bring the needle to the front at A, using the same hole.

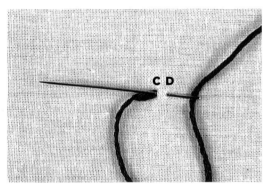

3 Pull the thread through. Again, with the thread below the needle, take the needle from C to B. Bring the needle to the back at D.

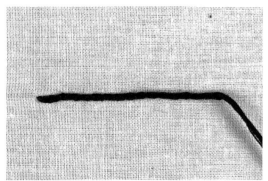

4 Pull the thread through. Continue stitching in the same sequence, always keeping the thread below the needle, and making the stitches the same length.

Straight Stitch (Circular)

This stitch is versatile, but the sample I have created here demonstrates how to do this stitch in a circular pattern that is used later in this book.

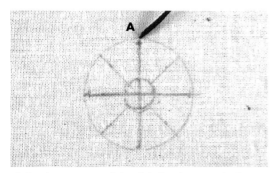

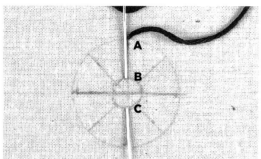

1 In the center of the fabric, draw a circle with a smaller circle in the center and four intersecting lines. Bring the thread to the front at A on the outer edge of the circle.

2 Take the thread to the back at B along the inner circle. Bring the thread to the front at C, on the outer edge of the circle opposite to the first stitch.

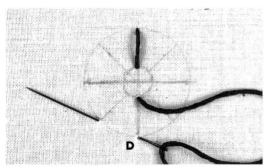

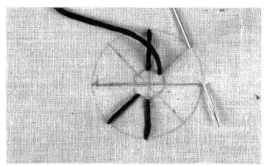

3 Pull the thread through. Take the needle to the back at D on the outer circle. Bring the needle to the front at E.

4 Continue the stitches in the same sequence with stitches opposite to each other, working around the circle.

5 Continue until the circle is filled. Optional: Add several French or colonial knots in the center.

Straight Stitch (Random)

A straight stitch with random placement and spacing is a fast way to fill a shape.

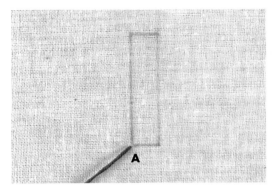

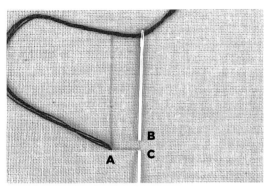

1 Draw the outline of the shape on the fabric. Bring the thread to the front at A on the outer edge of the shape.

2 Take the thread to the back at B, along the opposite edge of the shape. Bring the thread to the front at C on the outer edge of the shape above the first stitch.

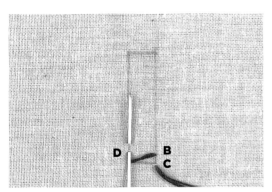

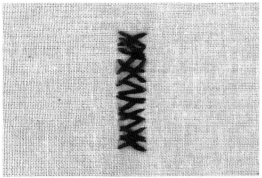

3 Pull the thread through. Take the needle to the back at D on the outer edge of the shape.

4 Continue the stitches in the same sequence, working with random spacing, and stitches opposite each other.

Waste Knot

Using a waste knot to start your embroidery is a clean way to keep the work neat on the back.

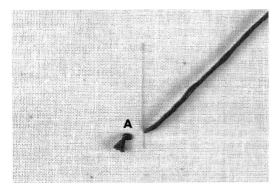

1 Knot the end of the thread. Take the needle to the back at A, a short distance from the line of the shape to be stitched. The waste knot will be on the front of the project.

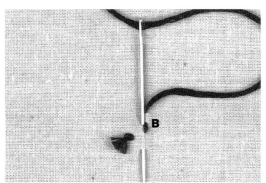

2 Take the thread to the back at point B along the line to be stitched. Add two backstitches to secure the thread.

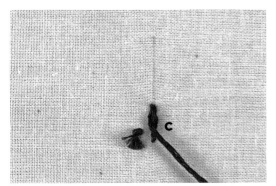

3 Take the needle to the front at C and proceed with the desired stitching along the line or shape. Stitch over the top of the two backstitches.

4 Cut off the waste knot. The thread is now secured in place without a bulky knot on the back of the project.

Watercolor Rainbow Hoop

This uplifting phrase with the painterly background may be displayed in a hoop and used as wall art in any room. This design may also be enlarged and easily adapted to a square throw pillow. For the text, copy and print the color diagram from this project.

Finished size: 8" x 8" (20.3 x 20.3cm) | Color diagram: page 61

Materials

- 12" x 12" (30.5 x 30.5cm) piece of natural muslin cotton
- 8" (20.3cm) round embroidery hoop
- Sticky Fabri-Solvy stabilizer, one letter-size sheet
- Water-soluble pen (blue)
- Watercolor or gouache paint set (basic assortment of six colors)
- Watercolor brush (round or flat in any size from 4 to 12)
- Paint palette (or other surface for mixing paint and water)
- Embroidery needle, size 2 to 4 (as preferred)
- Embroidery floss (one skein):
  - Black (DMC 310)

Instructions

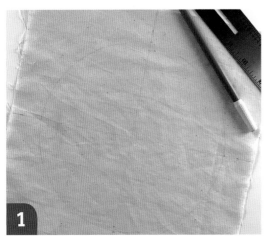

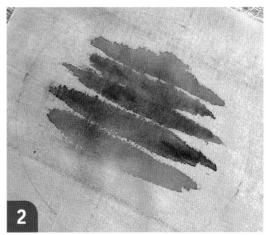

1 With the water-soluble pen, draw the centerlines on the fabric in both horizontal and vertical directions. Draw the outline of the hoop centered on the pen lines.

2 Mix small amounts of six watercolors or gouache paints keeping each color separate. The six suggested colors are yellow, orange, red, purple, blue, and green. With the brush, paint the lightest color first with a quick, loose brushstroke motion. These are painted "by eye" and do not need to be exact. Allow the paint to dry for two or three minutes.

In the meantime, thoroughly wash the brush with soap and water, then dry with a paper towel. Proceed with painting the next color and follow the same steps. Allow the paint to dry for a few hours before proceeding with stitching.

3 Print or photocopy the template on the sheet of Sticky Fabri-Solvy stabilizer. Remove the backing paper from the stabilizer sheet. Align the centerlines of the template with the pen lines placed on top of the dry watercolor brushstrokes. Gently press the adhesive side of the stabilizer sheet onto the fabric. Use a few straight pins to hold the stabilizer sheet firmly in place.

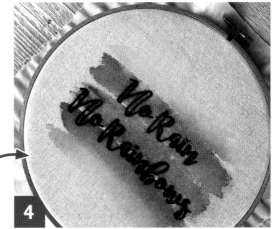

4 Insert the fabric into the hoop. Stitch the text.

5 Gently rinse the fabric under running water to remove the stabilizer. (Note: The painted brushstrokes will not run or wash out if submerged in water for a short time. Do not over wash.) Dry flat on a clean surface, such as a paper towel. After the fabric is dry, press it with a warm iron.

6 Insert the fabric into the hoop again. Adjust the screw post to be perfectly centered at the top. Finish the back of the hoop using one of the methods shown on pages 20 to 21.

Color Diagram
Copy at 140%

Text:
Stem stitch
Black (DMC 310)
6 strands

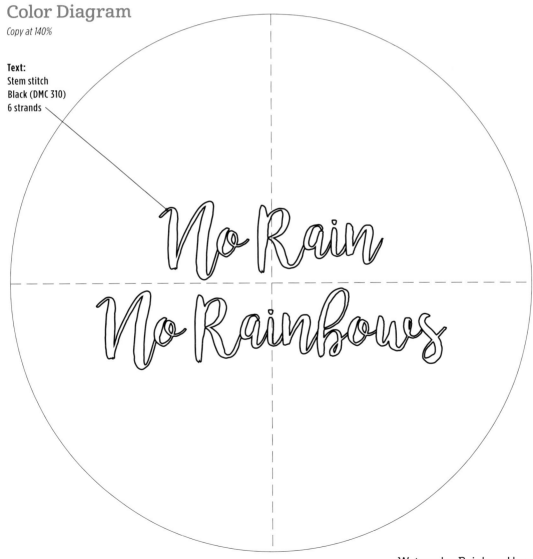

Floral Monogram Hoop

This feminine floral monogram stands alone as a design in a hoop for display on a wall. The design can also be applied to a pillowcase or tote bag. For a more ambitious project, you may put the letters together to spell out initials, a full name, or a word on larger-sized fabric. This could make a lovely framed wall decor for a little girl's bedroom or perhaps a romantic accent pillow. I suggest working out your design on paper first to determine the letter spacing and overall fabric size needed before beginning your stitching. Copy and print the alphabet from page 166 for this project.

Finished size: 6" x 6" (15.3 x 15.3cm) | Color diagram: page 65

Materials

- 8" x 8" (20.3 x 20.3cm) square of natural muslin, linen, or fabric of your choice
- 6" (15.3cm) round embroidery hoop
- Water-soluble pen (blue)
- Three 18" (45.7cm) lengths of ¼" (6mm)– wide light pink silk or polyester ribbon (Berwick Offray™ brand used in the sample)
- Embroidery needle, size 2 to 4 (as preferred)

- Chenille needle, size 18
- Embroidery floss (one skein each):
  - Very light cranberry (DMC 605)
  - Bright chartreuse (DMC 704)
  - Light peach (DMC 967)
  - Light yellow green (DMC 3348)
  - Medium melon (DMC 3706)
  - Pale pumpkin (DMC 3825)

Instructions

1

1 With the water-soluble pen, draw the centerlines on the fabric in both horizontal and vertical directions. Draw the outline of the hoop, centered on the pen lines. Trace the provided monogram template directly onto the fabric.

2

2 Insert the fabric into the hoop. Stitch the elements in the following sequence.
  1. Large and small leaves
  2. Large and small flowers (except ribbon roses)
  3. Letter outlines 1 and 2
  4. Ribbon rose spokes (Do not add the ribbon to the rose petals until the final step.)

3

3 Gently rinse the fabric under running water to remove the water-soluble pen lines. Dry flat on a clean surface, such as a paper towel. After the fabric is dry, press it with warm iron.

4

4 Insert the fabric into the hoop again. In this final step, add the spider web roses by weaving the ribbon through the spokes (see step by step on page 41). Adjust the screw post to be perfectly centered at the top. Finish the back of the hoop using one of the methods shown on pages 20 to 21.

Color Diagram

Copy at 100%

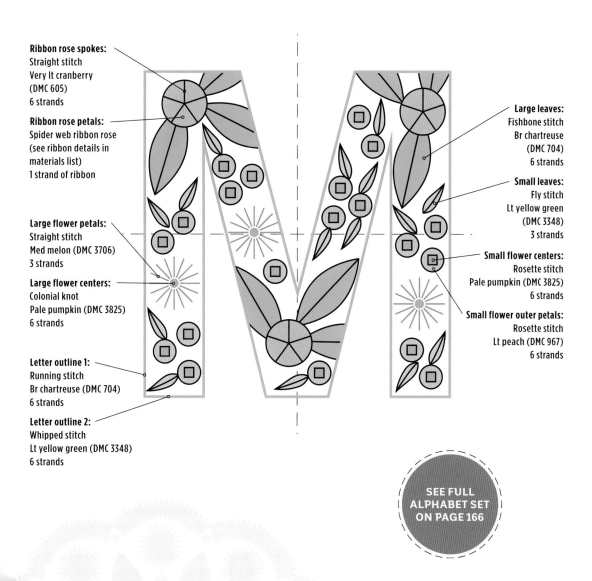

Ribbon rose spokes:
Straight stitch
Very lt cranberry
(DMC 605)
6 strands

Ribbon rose petals:
Spider web ribbon rose
(see ribbon details in
materials list)
1 strand of ribbon

Large flower petals:
Straight stitch
Med melon (DMC 3706)
3 strands

Large flower centers:
Colonial knot
Pale pumpkin (DMC 3825)
6 strands

Letter outline 1:
Running stitch
Br chartreuse (DMC 704)
6 strands

Letter outline 2:
Whipped stitch
Lt yellow green (DMC 3348)
6 strands

Large leaves:
Fishbone stitch
Br chartreuse
(DMC 704)
6 strands

Small leaves:
Fly stitch
Lt yellow green
(DMC 3348)
3 strands

Small flower centers:
Rosette stitch
Pale pumpkin (DMC 3825)
6 strands

Small flower outer petals:
Rosette stitch
Lt peach (DMC 967)
6 strands

SEE FULL ALPHABET SET ON PAGE 166

Mi Casa es Su Casa Hoop

This welcoming phrase stitched on fabric and displayed in a hoop can be used as wall art in a foyer or kitchen. In this sample, a vintage red plastic hoop from the 1960s was used. Look for old hoops in thrift shops, at flea markets, and from sellers online for a little something special. This design may also be enlarged and easily adapted to a square throw pillow. For the text, copy and print the color diagram from this project. Alternate designs are also available on page 69.

Finished size: 8" x 8" (20.3 x 20.3cm) | Color diagram: page 69

Materials

- 12" x 12" (30.5 x 30.5cm) natural muslin cotton
- 8" (20.3cm) round embroidery hoop
- Sticky Fabri-Solvy stabilizer, one letter-size sheet
- Water-soluble pen (blue)
- Embroidery needle, size 2 to 4 (as preferred)

- Embroidery floss (one skein each):
  - Red (DMC 321)
  - Medium cranberry (DMC 602)
  - Light beaver gray (DMC 648)
  - Very light aquamarine (DMC 993)
  - Pale pumpkin (DMC 3825)
- Embroidery floss (two skeins each):
  - Very light ash gray (DMC 535)
  - Ultra very light turquoise (DMC 3808)

Instructions

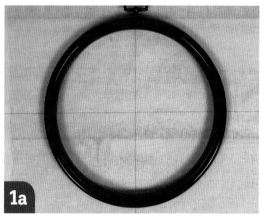

1a

1b

1 Print or photocopy the template on the sheet of Sticky Fabri-Solvy stabilizer. With the water-soluble pen, draw the centerlines on the fabric in both horizontal and vertical directions. Remove the backing paper from the stabilizer sheet. Align the centerlines of the template with the pen lines. Gently press the adhesive side of the stabilizer sheet onto the fabric. Use a few straight pins to hold the stabilizer sheet firmly in place.

2 Insert the fabric into the hoop. Stitch the elements in the following sequence.
 1. Text
 2. Flowers, stems, and leaves

3 Gently rinse the fabric under running water to remove the stabilizer. Dry flat on a clean surface, such as a paper towel. After the fabric is dry, press it with a warm iron.

4a

4b

4c

4 Insert the fabric into the hoop again. Adjust the screw post to be perfectly centered at the top. Finish the back of the hoop using the Fabric-Covered Back method shown on page 21.

Color Diagram

Copy at 200%

Flower G (color 2):
Satin stitch
Pale pumpkin
(DMC 3825)
6 strands

Small buds:
Straight stitch
Red (DMC 321)
6 strands

Dots (color 1):
French knots
Med cranberry
(DMC 602)
6 strands

Flower A:
Long and short stitch
in circular direction
Red (DMC 321)
6 strands

Leaves (color 1):
Satin stitch
Ultra very
lt turquoise
(DMC 3808)
6 strands

Flower G (color 1):
Satin stitch
Med cranberry
(DMC 602)
6 strands

Large buds:
Satin stitch
Red (DMC 321)
6 strands

Leaves (color 2):
Satin stitch
Very lt aquamarine
(DMC 993)
6 strands

Text:
Stem stitch in
double row
Very light ash gray
(DMC 535)
6 strands

Stems:
Stem stitch
Ultra very
lt turquoise
(DMC 3808)
6 strands

Flower B:
Long and short stitch in
circular direction
Pale pumpkin
(DMC 3825)
6 strands

Flower F:
Satin stitch
Red (DMC 321)
6 strands

Leaf stems (color 1):
Stem stitch
Lt beaver gray
(DMC 648)
3 strands

Flower E (color 1):
Satin stitch
Pale pumpkin
(DMC 3825)
6 strands

Flower E (color 2):
Satin stitch
Med cranberry
(DMC 602)
6 strands

Leaves (color 3):
Lazy daisy stitch
Lt beaver gray
(DMC 648)
3 strands

Dots (color 3):
French knots
Red (DMC 321)
6 strands

Dots (color 2):
French knots
Pale pumpkin
(DMC 3825)
6 strands

Flower D (color 1):
Satin stitch
Red (DMC 321)
6 strands

Flower D (color 2):
Satin stitch
Med cranberry
(DMC 602)
6 strands

Flower C:
Satin stitch
Med cranberry
(DMC 602)
6 strands

Leaves (color 4):
Lazy daisy stitch
Pale pumpkin
(DMC 3825)
3 strands

Leaf stem (color 2):
Stem stitch
Pale pumpkin
(DMC 3825)
3 strands

ALTERNATE
DESIGNS
Copy at 400%

Question Mark Art Hoop

This random abundance of French knots is a fun way to fill a letter or shape and turn it into an art piece. In this sample, a vintage green plastic hoop from the 1960s was used. Look for old hoops in thrift shops, at flea markets, and from sellers online for a personal touch. This idea can be applied to designs of your own creation. Alternate designs are also available on page 73.

Finished size: 3" x 4" (7.6 x 10.2cm) | Color diagram: page 73

Materials

- 8" x 8" (20.3 x 20.3cm) piece of 100% white cotton
- 6" (15.2cm) round embroidery hoop (for working)
- 3" x 4" (7.6 x 10.2cm) oval hoop or substitute a 4" (10.2cm) round hoop (for display)
- Sticky Fabri-Solvy stabilizer, one letter-size sheet
- Water-soluble pen (blue)
- Embroidery needle, size 2 to 4 (as preferred)
- Embroidery floss (one skein each):
  - Red (DMC 321)
  - Blue (DMC 336)
  - Green (DMC 699)
  - Medium tangerine (DMC 741)
  - Dark cyclamen pink (DMC 3804)
  - Dark bright turquoise (DMC 3844)

Instructions

1 Print or photocopy the template on the sheet of Sticky Fabri-Solvy stabilizer. With the water-soluble pen, draw the centerlines on the fabric in both horizontal and vertical directions. Remove the backing paper from the stabilizer sheet. Align the centerlines of the template with the pen lines. Gently press the adhesive side of the stabilizer sheet onto the fabric. Use a few straight pins to hold the stabilizer sheet firmly in place.

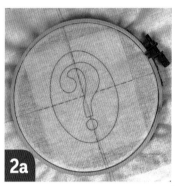
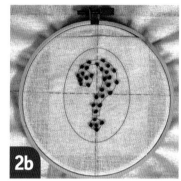
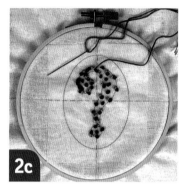

2 Insert the fabric into a 6" (15.2cm) round embroidery hoop for working. Stitch all the French knots by color. It will save time to stitch all the green knots, all the blue knots, etc. Fill in extra knots where necessary to compactly fill the design. Since the design has a random arrangement of knots, it will not matter if extra knots are squeezed in to fill sparser areas.

3 Gently rinse the fabric under running water to remove water-soluble pen lines. Dry flat on a clean surface, such as a paper towel. After the fabric is dry, press it with a warm iron.

4 Insert the fabric into the smaller oval or round hoop for display. Adjust the screw post to be perfectly centered at the top. Finish the back of the hoop using one of the methods shown on pages 20 to 21.

Color Diagram

Copy at 100%

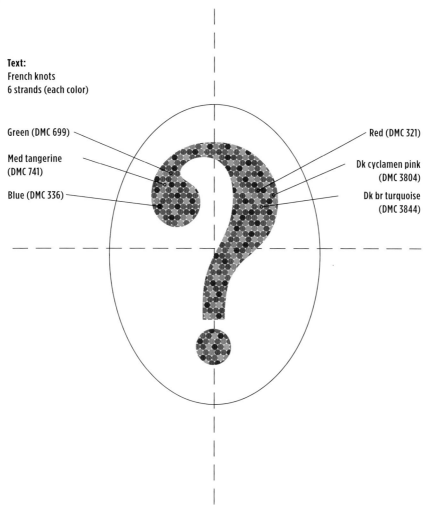

Text:
French knots
6 strands (each color)

Green (DMC 699)

Med tangerine
(DMC 741)

Blue (DMC 336)

Red (DMC 321)

Dk cyclamen pink
(DMC 3804)

Dk br turquoise
(DMC 3844)

ALTERNATE DESIGNS *Copy at 300%*

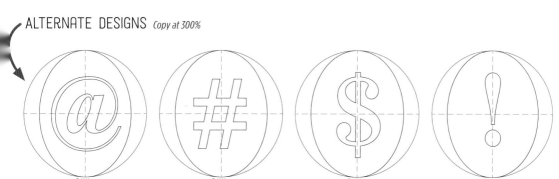

Fold Line · Fold Line · Fold Line · Fold Line

Life Is Too Short to Drink Cheap Champagne Oval Hoop

Life is too short to drink cheap champagne (or wine or beer)! The bubbles are embellished with little pearl beads. In this sample, a vintage oval hoop was used for a unique shape and look. You can find old embroidery hoops in thrift shops, at flea markets, and from sellers online. This project can be formatted in a round hoop as well as displayed in a picture frame. This design may also be enlarged and easily adapted to a throw pillow. An alternate design is also available on page 77.

Finished size: 8" x 10" (20.3 x 25.4cm) | Color diagram: page 77

Materials

- 12" x 14" (30.5 x 35.6cm) piece of quilt fabric (color and design of your choice)
- 8" (20.3cm) round embroidery hoop (for working)
- 8" x 10" (20.3 x 25.4cm) oval hoop (for display), or if you cannot find an oval hoop, substitute an 8" (20.3cm) round hoop
- Sticky Fabri-Solvy stabilizer, one letter-size sheet
- Water-soluble pen (blue)

- 4mm-diameter pearl beads (sold in bulk pack)
- White sewing thread and needle
- Embroidery needle, size 2 to 4 (as preferred)
- Embroidery floss (1 skein each):
  - Dark beaver gray (DMC 646)
  - Medium old gold (DMC 729)
  - Dark hunter green (DMC 3345)
  - Light mahogany (DMC 3776)
  - Very dark terra-cotta (DMC 3777)

Instructions

2 Insert the fabric into an 8" (20.3cm) round embroidery hoop for working. Stitch the elements in the following sequence.
1. Text
2. Bottle, glass, and flourishes

1 Print or photocopy the template on the sheet of Sticky Fabri-Solvy stabilizer. With the water-soluble pen, draw the centerlines on the fabric in both horizontal and vertical directions. Remove the backing paper from the stabilizer sheet. Align the centerlines of the template with the pen lines. Gently press the adhesive side of the stabilizer sheet onto the fabric. Use a few straight pins to hold the stabilizer sheet firmly in place.

3 Sew the pearl beads in place with white thread and a sewing needle.

4 Gently rinse the fabric under running water to remove the stabilizer. Dry flat on a clean surface, such as a paper towel. After the fabric is dry, press it with a warm iron, taking care not to iron over the beads.

5 Insert the fabric into the hoop again. Adjust the screw post to be perfectly centered at the top. Finish the back of the hoop using one of the methods shown on pages 20 to 21.

Color Diagram

Copy at 200%

Text outline:
Stem stitch
Very dk terra-cotta
(DMC 3777)
3 strands

Champagne bottle (top):
Long and short stitch
Med old gold (DMC 729)
6 strands

Text fill:
Stem stitch
Lt mahogany
(DMC 3776)
3 strands

Champagne bottle (label):
Long and short stitch
Dk beaver gray (DMC 646)
6 strands

Flourishes:
Stem stitch
Lt mahogany
(DMC 3776)
6 strands

Champagne bottle (glass):
Long and short stitch
Dk hunter green
(DMC 3345)
6 strands

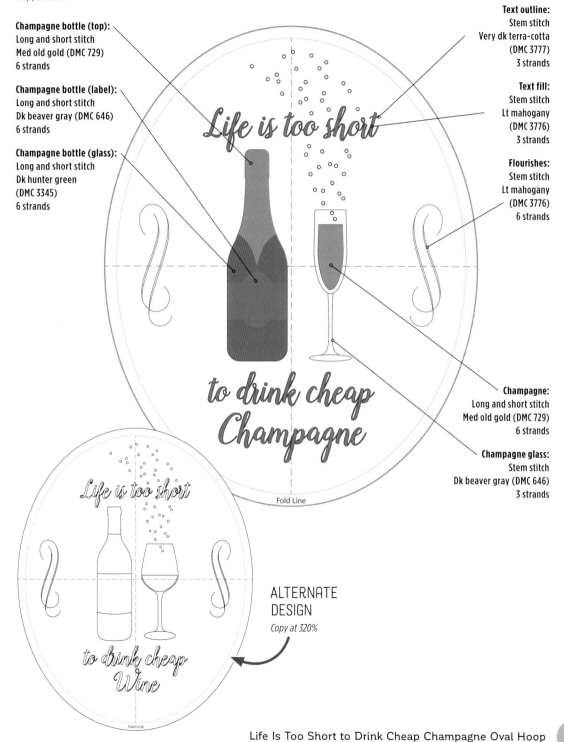

Fold Line

Champagne:
Long and short stitch
Med old gold (DMC 729)
6 strands

Champagne glass:
Stem stitch
Dk beaver gray (DMC 646)
3 strands

ALTERNATE
DESIGN
Copy at 320%

Fold Line

Life Is Too Short to Drink Cheap Champagne Oval Hoop

My Happy Place Frame

This cheerful phrase with a cloud-shaped border is appealing to children and adults alike. It makes a nice framed plaque for a bedroom, den, or nook, and would look great placed on a table or hung on a wall. The border is embellished with buttons that can be multicolored, as shown, or all in a single color. This template may also be enlarged and easily adapted to a lumbar or square throw pillow. For the text, copy and print the color diagram from this project. An alternate design is also available on page 81.

Finished size: 5" x 7" (12.7 x 17.8cm) | Color diagram: page 81

Materials

- 12" x 12" (30.5 x 30.5cm) piece of natural muslin cotton
- 6" (15.2cm) round embroidery hoop
- Sticky Fabri-Solvy stabilizer, one letter-size sheet
- Water-soluble pen (blue)
- ¼" (6mm) buttons in assorted colors
- 5" x 7" (12.7 x 17.8cm) picture frame with glass
- Embroidery needle, size 2 to 4 (as preferred)

- Embroidery floss (1 skein each):
  - Dark lavender (DMC 209)
  - Light avocado green (DMC 470)
  - Ultra light avocado green (DMC 472)
  - Light turquoise (DMC 598)
  - Plum (DMC 718)
  - Medium tangerine (DMC 741)
  - Dark cornflower blue (DMC 792)
  - Medium melon (DMC 3706)
  - Dark bright turquoise (DMC 3844)
- 5" x 7" (12.7 x 17.8cm) piece of thin cardboard
- ½" (12.7mm)–wide masking or drafting tape

Instructions

1 Print or photocopy the template on the sheet of Sticky Fabri-Solvy stabilizer. With the water-soluble pen, draw the centerlines on the fabric in both horizontal and vertical directions. Remove the backing paper from the stabilizer sheet. Align the centerlines of the template with the pen lines. Gently press the adhesive side of stabilizer sheet onto the fabric. Use a few straight pins to hold the stabilizer sheet firmly in place.

2 Insert the fabric into the hoop. Stitch the elements in the following sequence.
1. Text
2. Borders

After doing all the stitching, sew the buttons around the border on the designated circles in alternating colors.

3 Gently rinse the fabric under running water to remove the stabilizer. Dry flat on a clean surface, such as a paper towel. After the fabric is dry, press it with a warm iron.

4 Dissemble the picture frame and clean the glass. Center the stitched fabric onto the cardboard. Wrap the excess fabric onto the backside and trim off excess fabric. Secure with tape. Assemble the frame.

Color Diagram

Copy at 150%

Text:
Satin stitch (thick strokes)
Stem stitch (thin strokes)

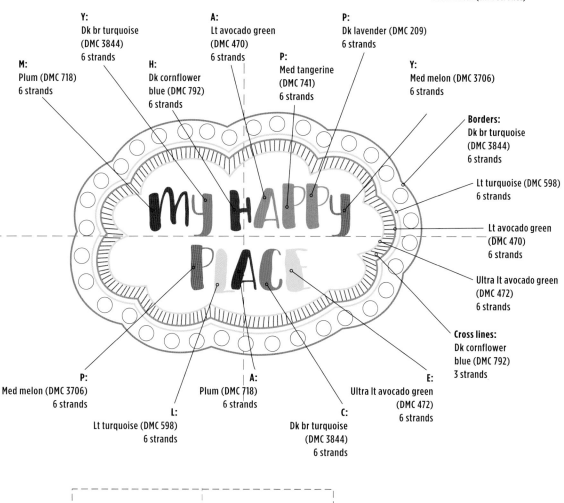

Y:
Dk br turquoise
(DMC 3844)
6 strands

A:
Lt avocado green
(DMC 470)
6 strands

P:
Dk lavender (DMC 209)
6 strands

M:
Plum (DMC 718)
6 strands

H:
Dk cornflower
blue (DMC 792)
6 strands

P:
Med tangerine
(DMC 741)
6 strands

Y:
Med melon (DMC 3706)
6 strands

Borders:
Dk br turquoise
(DMC 3844)
6 strands

Lt turquoise (DMC 598)
6 strands

Lt avocado green
(DMC 470)
6 strands

Ultra lt avocado green
(DMC 472)
6 strands

Cross lines:
Dk cornflower
blue (DMC 792)
3 strands

P:
Med melon (DMC 3706)
6 strands

A:
Plum (DMC 718)
6 strands

E:
Ultra lt avocado green
(DMC 472)
6 strands

L:
Lt turquoise (DMC 598)
6 strands

C:
Dk br turquoise
(DMC 3844)
6 strands

Fold Line

ALTERNATE
DESIGN
Copy at 250%

International Symbol of Welcome

The pineapple has been recognized as the international symbol of welcome, friendship, and hospitality for centuries, dating back to the 1400s. There is no better way to receive visitors in your home than with a hand-stitched welcome sign featuring the once rare and exotic crowned fruit. Change the colors of the design to suit your taste. Choose a picture frame to match your home décor and hang proudly in the foyer or living room. This would make a very sweet gift for a new homeowner. Copy and print the alphabet from page 167 for this project.

Finished size: 8" x 10" (20.3 x 25.4cm) | Color diagram: page 85

Materials

- 12" x 14" (30.5cm x 35.7cm) piece of natural unbleached muslin cotton
- 8" (20.3cm) round embroidery hoop
- Sticky Fabri-Solvy stabilizer, one letter-size sheet
- Water-soluble pen (blue)
- Picture frame with glass, 8" x 10" (20.3 x 25.4cm)
- Thin cardboard, 1 piece, 8" x 10" (20.3 x 25.4cm)
- Masking or drafting tape, ½" (12.7mm)–wide

- Embroidery needle, size 2 to 4 (as preferred)
- Embroidery floss (one skein each):
  - Brown (DMC 779)
  - Dark burnt orange (DMC 900)
  - Dark hunter green (DMC 3345)
  - Hunter green (DMC 3346)
  - Medium yellow green (DMC 3347)
  - Light yellow green (DMC 3348)
  - Dark autumn gold (DMC 3853)
  - Medium autumn gold (DMC 3854)
  - Light autumn gold (DMC 3855)
  - Ultra very light mahogany (3856)

Instructions

1a

1b

1 Print or photocopy the template on the sheet of Sticky Fabri-Solvy stabilizer. With the water-soluble pen, draw the centerlines on the fabric in both horizontal and vertical directions. Remove the backing paper from the stabilizer sheet. Align the centerlines of the template with the pen lines. Gently press the adhesive side of the stabilizer sheet onto the fabric.

2a

2b

2c

2 Insert the fabric into the hoop. Stitch the elements in the following sequence.
1. Text
2. Pineapple base
3. Leaves
4. Border

3 Gently rinse the fabric under running water to remove the stabilizer. Dry flat on a clean surface, such as a paper towel. After the fabric is dry, press it with a warm iron.

SEE FULL
ALPHABET
SET FOR THE
NAME DROP ON
PAGE 167

4 Disassemble the picture frame and clean the glass. Center the stitched fabric onto the cardboard. Wrap the excess fabric onto the backside and trim off any excess fabric. Secure with tape.

Color Diagram *Copy at 250%*

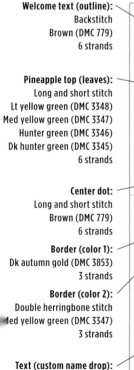

Welcome text (outline):
Backstitch
Brown (DMC 779)
6 strands

Pineapple top (leaves):
Long and short stitch
Lt yellow green (DMC 3348)
Med yellow green (DMC 3347)
Hunter green (DMC 3346)
Dk hunter green (DMC 3345)
6 strands

Center dot:
Long and short stitch
Brown (DMC 779)
6 strands

Border (color 1):
Dk autumn gold (DMC 3853)
3 strands

Border (color 2):
Double herringbone stitch
Med yellow green (DMC 3347)
3 strands

Text (custom name drop):
Stem stitch
Brown (DMC 779)
6 strands

Welcome text (fill):
Straight stitch
Stitches 1 and 2: Ultra very lt mahogany (3856)
Stitches 3 and 4: Med autumn gold (DMC 3854)
Stitches 5 and 6: Dk autumn gold (DMC 3853)
Stitches 7 and 8: Dk burnt orange (DMC 900)
6 strands

Pineapple outline:
Stem stitch
Brown (DMC 779)
6 strands

Pineapple bottom (fill):
Straight stitch
Rows 1 and 2: Lt autumn gold (DMC 3855)
Rows 3 and 4: Ultra very lt mahogany (3856)
Rows 5 and 6: Med autumn gold (DMC 3854)
Rows 7 and 8: Dk autumn gold (DMC 3853)
Rows 9 and 10: Dk burnt orange (DMC 900)
6 strands

Commemorative Motherhood Frame

Honor a mother you love by stitching this commemorative plaque with the date she became a mother. This is a nice gift for a mother-to-be as a baby shower gift, or as a new or established mother for Mother's Day. The light letters and colorful flowers on a dark fabric create a vintage chalkboard look. It makes a nice framed piece for a bedroom, den, or nook, placed on a table or hung on a wall. Copy and print the color diagram and customize the date needed with the numbers provided by tracing them onto the stabilizer.

Finished size: 5" x 7" (12.7 x 17.8cm) | Color diagram: page 89

Materials:

- 12" x 12" (30.5 x 30.5cm) black cotton
- 6" (15.2cm) round embroidery hoop
- Sticky Fabri-Solvy stabilizer, one letter-size sheet
- Water-soluble marking pencil (white)
- 5" x 7" (12.7 x 17.8cm) picture frame with glass
- 5" x 7" (12.7 x 17.8cm) thin cardboard
- Masking or drafting tape, ½" (12.7mm)–wide masking or drafting tape

- Embroidery needle, size 2 to 4 (as preferred)
- Embroidery floss (one skein each):
  - Ecru (DMC Ecru)
  - Dark lavender (DMC 209)
  - Medium cranberry (DMC 602)
  - Chartreuse (DMC 703)
  - Medium tangerine (DMC 741)
  - Medium yellow (DMC 743)

Instructions

1 Print or photocopy the template on the sheet of Sticky Fabri-Solvy stabilizer. With the water-soluble pencil, draw the centerlines on the fabric in both horizontal and vertical directions. Remove the backing paper from the stabilizer sheet. Align the centerlines of the template with the white pencil lines. Gently press the adhesive side of the stabilizer sheet onto the fabric. Use a few straight pins to hold the stabilizer sheet firmly in place.

2 Insert the fabric into the hoop. Stitch the elements in the following sequence.
  1. Text outlines   2. Text fills   3. Flowers

3 Gently rinse the fabric under running water to remove the stabilizer. Dry flat on a clean surface, such as a paper towel. After the fabric is dry, press it with a warm iron.

4 Disassemble the picture frame and clean the glass. Center the stitched fabric onto the cardboard. Wrap the excess fabric onto the backside and trim off any excess fabric. Secure with tape, then assemble the frame.

Color Diagram *Copy at 200%*

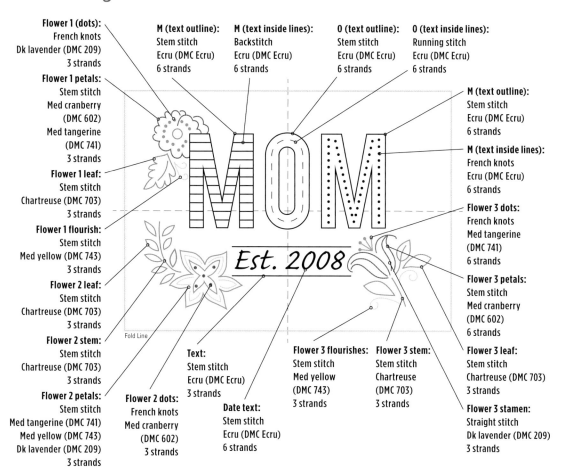

Flower 1 (dots):
French knots
Dk lavender (DMC 209)
3 strands

Flower 1 petals:
Stem stitch
Med cranberry
(DMC 602)
Med tangerine
(DMC 741)
3 strands

Flower 1 leaf:
Stem stitch
Chartreuse (DMC 703)
3 strands

Flower 1 flourish:
Stem stitch
Med yellow (DMC 743)
3 strands

Flower 2 leaf:
Stem stitch
Chartreuse (DMC 703)
3 strands

Flower 2 stem:
Stem stitch
Chartreuse (DMC 703)
3 strands

Flower 2 petals:
Stem stitch
Med tangerine (DMC 741)
Med yellow (DMC 743)
Dk lavender (DMC 209)
3 strands

M (text outline):
Stem stitch
Ecru (DMC Ecru)
6 strands

M (text inside lines):
Backstitch
Ecru (DMC Ecru)
6 strands

O (text outline):
Stem stitch
Ecru (DMC Ecru)
6 strands

O (text inside lines):
Running stitch
Ecru (DMC Ecru)
6 strands

M (text outline):
Stem stitch
Ecru (DMC Ecru)
6 strands

M (text inside lines):
French knots
Ecru (DMC Ecru)
6 strands

Flower 3 dots:
French knots
Med tangerine
(DMC 741)
6 strands

Flower 3 petals:
Stem stitch
Med cranberry
(DMC 602)
6 strands

Flower 3 leaf:
Stem stitch
Chartreuse (DMC 703)
3 strands

Flower 3 stamen:
Straight stitch
Dk lavender (DMC 209)
3 strands

Flower 2 dots:
French knots
Med cranberry
(DMC 602)
3 strands

Text:
Stem stitch
Ecru (DMC Ecru)
3 strands

Date text:
Stem stitch
Ecru (DMC Ecru)
6 strands

Flower 3 flourishes:
Stem stitch
Med yellow
(DMC 743)
3 strands

Flower 3 stem:
Stem stitch
Chartreuse
(DMC 703)
3 strands

Fold Line

1 2 3 4 5 6 7 8 9 0

ALTERNATE
DESIGN
Copy at 200%

Classic Cocktail Coasters

These elegant hand-stitched coasters feature classic cocktail recipes. The fabric is absorbent and functional. This set dresses up any cocktail party or makes a nice keepsake gift for a special hostess. Feel free to vary the colors to fit your taste. For the text, copy and print the color diagrams from this project. Alternate designs are also available on page 93.

Finished size: 4¼" x 4¼" (10.8 x 10.8cm) each | Color diagrams: page 93

Materials

- Two pieces of 5" x 20" (25.4 x 50.8cm) natural muslin, linen, or fabric of your choice to make set of four coasters (natural linen is used here)
- 6" (15.2cm) round embroidery hoop
- Sticky Fabri-Solvy stabilizer, one letter-size sheet
- Water-soluble pen (blue)
- Embroidery needle, size 2 to 4 (as preferred)
- Embroidery floss (one skein each):
  - Very light ash gray (DMC 535)
  - Plum (DMC 718)
  - Dark melon (DMC 3705)
  - Very dark sea green (DMC 3812)
  - Dark lavender blue (DMC 3838)

Manhattan

2 oz ... bourbon
1 oz ... vermouth
2 dashes bitters

Cuba Libre

2 oz white rum
4 oz cola
1/2 oz lime juice

Martini

2 oz gin or vodka
1 oz vermouth
1 olive

Daiquiri

2 oz white rum
1 oz lime juice
3/4 oz simple syrup

Instructions

1 Print or photocopy all four coaster templates together on the sheet of Sticky Fabri-Solvy stabilizer. Cut the templates into four separate pieces, leaving an extra margin outside the final cutting lines. With the water-soluble pen, draw the centerlines on the fabric in both horizontal and vertical directions. Remove the backing paper from one of the four stabilizer pieces. Then align the centerlines of the template with the pen lines. Gently press the adhesive side of the stabilizer piece onto the fabric. Repeat the same process with the remaining three templates, leaving about ½" (1.3cm) in between each coaster. Use a few straight pins to hold each stabilizer piece firmly in place.

2 Insert the fabric into the hoop. Stitch the elements on each coaster in the following sequence. Use extra small backstitches for the recipe text since the lettering is very fine.
1. Title text
2. Recipe text

IMPORTANT NOTE:
DO NOT STITCH THE BORDERS UNTIL STEP 3.

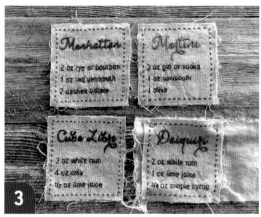

3 Place the other linen fabric piece back-to-back with the right sides facing out and the edges neatly aligned. Pin together with straight pins. Stitch the borders of each coaster, sewing together through both thicknesses of fabric.

4 Cut the fabric along the cutting lines of each coaster template. Gently rinse the coasters under running water to remove the stabilizer. Dry flat on a clean surface, such as a paper towel. After the fabric is dry, press it with a warm iron. Fray the edges of each coaster by removing several threads along each edge.

Color Diagrams

Copy at 170%

Border (color 1):
Running stitch
Very lt ash gray (DMC 535)
6 strands

Border (color 2):
Whipped running stitch
Plum (DMC 718)
6 strands

Recipe Text:
Backstitch
Very lt ash gray (DMC 535)
3 strands

Title Text:
Stem stitch
Plum (DMC 718)
3 strands

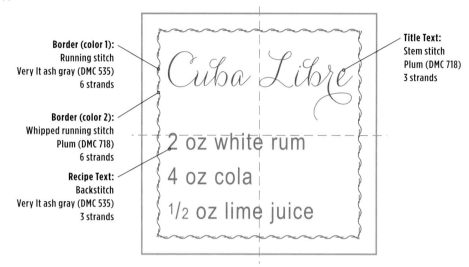

Copy at 240%

Title Text and Border (color 2):
Dk lavender blue (DMC 3838)

Title Text and Border (color 2):
Dk melon (DMC 3705)

Title Text and Border (color 2):
Very dk sea green (DMC 3812)

ALTERNATE DESIGNS *Copy at 320%*

Days of the Week Tea Towels

A fresh tea towel for each day of the week will beautify any home. Seven charming designs feature retro-style kitchen utensil icons in a colorful assortment for each day. Quilt fabric scraps or cuts from fat quarters are used as appliqués to towels. Linen, flour sack, waffle, and terry cloth off-the-shelf towels may be used, and are easily found in bulk packs online or at your favorite retailer. Copy and print the color diagrams from this project.

Finished size: 13" x 22" (33 x 55.9cm) | Color diagrams: pages 97 to 99

Materials:

- Seven 13" x 22" (33 x 55.9cm) tea towels, linen or cotton (or similar size)
- 8" (20.3cm) round embroidery hoop
- Sticky Fabri-Solvy stabilizer, four letter-size sheets (yields two towels per sheet)
- Water-soluble pen (blue)
- Seven pieces of 7" x 7" (17.8 x 17.8cm) scraps of quilt cotton in assorted colors, one each per tea towel
- Embroidery needle, size 2 to 4 (as preferred)

- Embroidery floss (1 skein each) as listed, or modify to match quilt fabrics:
  - Black (DMC 310)
  - Violet (DMC 553)
  - Medium cranberry (DMC 602)
  - Bright chartreuse (DMC 704)
  - Tangerine (DMC 740)
  - Dark blue (DMC 825)
  - Dark melon (DMC 3705)
  - Medium bright turquoise (DMC 3845)

Instructions

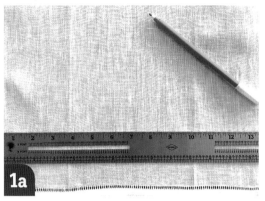

1 Print or photocopy two templates together per sheet on the four sheets of Sticky Fabri-Solvy stabilizer. Cut the templates into seven separate pieces with scissors, leaving an extra margin outside the final cutting lines. With the water-soluble pen, draw the centerline on each tea towel in the vertical direction. Draw a horizontal line approximately 1" (2.5cm) above the hemline on the front of the towel. This position may vary depending on the particular towels. Remove the backing paper from one of the seven stabilizer pieces.

Using one piece of quilt fabric, place the fabric face down onto the stabilizer where the icon is positioned. Align the centerlines of the template with the pen lines. Gently press the adhesive side of the stabilizer piece onto the fabric. Use a few straight pins to hold each stabilizer piece firmly in place. Repeat the same process with the remaining six templates.

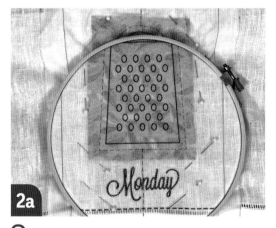

2 Insert the first tea towel into the hoop. Stitch the elements in the following sequence.
1. Icon outline
2. Text
Repeat the same process with the remaining six templates.

3 Gently rinse each tea towel under running water to remove the stabilizer. Dry flat on a clean surface, such as a paper towel. After the fabric is dry, press it with a warm iron.

4 As the final step, choose a floss color that closely matches the text. Stitch around each appliqué with a blanket stitch going through both layers of the quilt fabric and towel for a sturdy finished edge.

Color Diagram

Copy at 180%

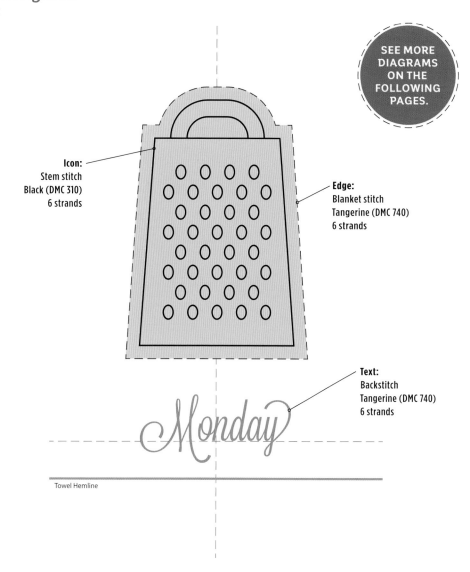

SEE MORE DIAGRAMS ON THE FOLLOWING PAGES.

Icon:
Stem stitch
Black (DMC 310)
6 strands

Edge:
Blanket stitch
Tangerine (DMC 740)
6 strands

Text:
Backstitch
Tangerine (DMC 740)
6 strands

Monday

Towel Hemline

Color Diagrams *Copy at 250%*

Icon:
Stem stitch
Black (DMC 310)
6 strands

Edge:
Blanket stitch
Violet (DMC 553)
6 strands

Text:
Backstitch
Violet (DMC 553)
6 strands

Tuesday

Towel Hemline

Icon:
Stem stitch
Black (DMC 310)
6 strands

Edge:
Blanket stitch
Dk melon
(DMC 3705)
6 strands

Text:
Backstitch
Dk melon
(DMC 3705)
6 strands

Wednesday

Towel Hemline

Edge:
Blanket stitch
Br chartreuse (DMC 704)
6 strands

Icon:
Stem stitch
Black (DMC 310)
6 strands

Text:
Backstitch
Br chartreuse (DMC 704)
6 strands

Thursday

Towel Hemline

Color Diagrams *Copy at 250%*

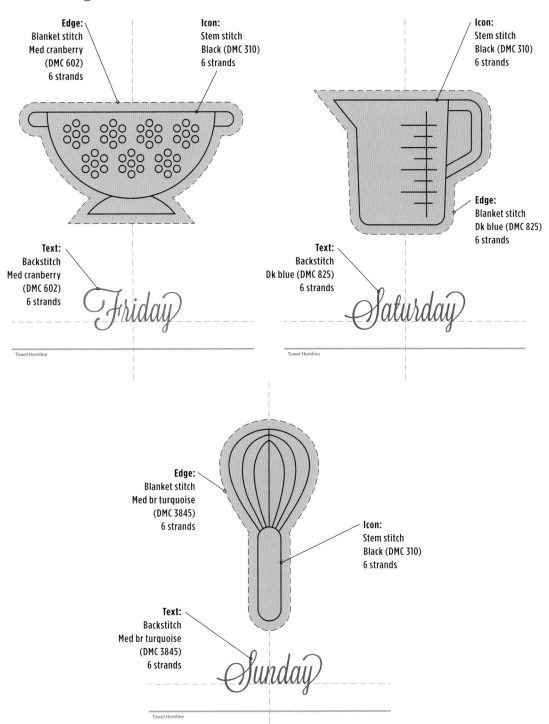

Edge:
Blanket stitch
Med cranberry
(DMC 602)
6 strands

Icon:
Stem stitch
Black (DMC 310)
6 strands

Icon:
Stem stitch
Black (DMC 310)
6 strands

Friday

Text:
Backstitch
Med cranberry
(DMC 602)
6 strands

Towel Hemline

Saturday

Text:
Backstitch
Dk blue (DMC 825)
6 strands

Edge:
Blanket stitch
Dk blue (DMC 825)
6 strands

Towel Hemline

Edge:
Blanket stitch
Med br turquoise
(DMC 3845)
6 strands

Icon:
Stem stitch
Black (DMC 310)
6 strands

Text:
Backstitch
Med br turquoise
(DMC 3845)
6 strands

Sunday

Towel Hemline

Always Kiss Me Pillowcase Set

Sweet romantic sentiments stitched on pillowcase edges make a wonderful wedding gift for newlyweds. Make this project in the color scheme you prefer. The templates provided will fit on the cuff edge of either a standard- or king-size case of your choice. For the text, copy and print the color diagrams from this project. Alternate designs are also available on page 103.

Finished size of design: 3" x 11" (7.6 x 28cm) | Color diagrams: page 103

Materials

- Set of two pillowcases (standard or king-size)
- 6" (15.2cm) round embroidery hoop
- Sticky Fabri-Solvy stabilizer, one letter-size sheet
- Water-soluble pen (blue)
- Embroidery needle, size 2 to 4 (as preferred)
- Embroidery floss (1 skein each):
    - Medium blue (DMC 311)
    - Light blue (DMC 813)
    - Very light aquamarine (DMC 993)
    - Very dark sea green (DMC 3812)

Instructions

1 Print or photocopy two templates together on one sheet of Sticky Fabri-Solvy stabilizer. Cut the templates into two separate pieces with scissors. With the water-soluble pen, draw centerlines on the finished cuff edge of each pillowcase in both horizontal and vertical directions. Remove the backing paper from one of the two stabilizer pieces. Align the centerlines of the template with the pen lines. Gently press the adhesive side of the stabilizer piece onto the fabric. Use a few straight pins to hold the stabilizer sheet firmly in place. Repeat same process with remaining template.

2 Insert the fabric into the hoop. Stitch the elements in the following sequence.
　1. Text
　2. Icons

3 Gently rinse each tea towel under running water to remove the stabilizer. Dry flat on a clean surface, such as a paper towel. After the fabric is dry, press it with a warm iron.

Color Diagrams *Copy at 200%*

Star icon (color 1):
Star stitch
Lt blue (DMC 813)
6 strands

Text:
Stem stitch and French knots
Med blue (DMC 311)
3 strands

Star icon (color 2):
Star stitch
Very lt aquamarine
(DMC 993)
6 strands

Text:Star icon (color 3):
Star stitch
Very dk sea green
(DMC 3812)
6 strands

Always Kiss Me Good Morning

Always Kiss Me Good Night

ALTERNATE DESIGNS *Copy at 200%*

I Belong With You

You Belong With Me

Magic Lumbar Accent Pillow

This charming pillow can be used on a bed or sofa. It makes a wonderful wedding gift for newlyweds or for any couple. This project is also easily adapted to a square pillow. Make this project in the color scheme you prefer depending on the pillowcase. Ready-made lumbar pillowcases in a wide variety of colors and fabrics are easily found online or at your favorite retailer. For the text, copy and print the color diagram from this project. An alternate design is also available on page 107.

Finished size: 12" x 18" (30.5 x 45.7cm) | Color diagram: page 107

Materials

- One ready-made pillowcase, lumbar, or fabric square of your choice
- 6" (15.2cm) or 8" (20.3cm) round embroidery hoop
- Sticky Fabri-Solvy stabilizer, one letter-size sheet
- Water-soluble pen (blue)
- Embroidery needle, size 2 to 4 (as preferred)
- Embroidery floss (1 skein each):
  - White (DMC Blanc)
  - Black (DMC 310)
  - Plum (DMC 718)
  - Gold metallic (DMC E3821)

This is where the *Magic* happens ♡

Instructions

1 Print or photocopy the template on the sheet of Sticky Fabri-Solvy stabilizer. With the water-soluble pen, draw the centerlines on the pillowcase in both horizontal and vertical directions. Remove the backing paper from the stabilizer sheet. Align the centerlines of the template with the pen lines. Gently press the adhesive side of stabilizer sheet onto the fabric. Use a few straight pins to hold the stabilizer sheet firmly in place.

2 Insert the fabric into the hoop. Stitch the elements in the following sequence.
   1. Text
   2. Icons

3 Gently rinse the pillowcase under running water to remove the stabilizer. Dry flat on a clean surface, such as a paper towel. After the pillowcase is dry, press it with a warm iron.

Color Diagram *Copy at 250%*

This is where the

Magic

happens

xoxo

Small text:
Stem stitch
Black (DMC 310)
6 strands

Large text:
Stem stitch
Plum (DMC 718)
6 strands

Large text outline:
Stem stitch
White (DMC Blanc)
6 strands

Heart and XOXO icons:
Stem stitch
Gold metallic (DMC E3821)
6 strands

Naughty
xoxo
& Nice

ALTERNATE
DESIGN
Copy at 300%

"Stop" Brick Doorstop

Don't use a basic doorstop from the hardware store. This doorstop makes one of the best home accessories you never knew you needed. Brick is an ideal material for this project due to its weight, but it needs a fabric cover so it doesn't scratch the door or floor. When not in use, just push it to the side of the door with your foot. It really works well as a hands-free solution! For the text, copy and print the color diagram from this project. Alternate designs are also available on page 113.

Finished size: 4" x 8" x 2¾" (10.2 x 20.3 x 7cm) | Color diagram: page 112

Materials

- 14" x 18" (35.6 x 45.7cm) piece of black cotton duck cloth or canvas
- 8" (20.3cm) round embroidery hoop
- Sticky Fabri-Solvy stabilizer, one letter-size sheet
- Water-soluble marking pencil (white)
- 4" x 8" x 2¾" (10.2 x 20.3 x 7cm) or similar-size standard brick
- Plastic food wrap

- White glue
- Embroidery needle, size 2 to 4 (as preferred)
- Embroidery floss (one skein each):
  - Ultra light avocado green (DMC 472)
  - Medium orange spice (DMC 721)
  - Light tangerine (DMC 742)
  - Dark cyclamen pink (DMC 3804)
  - Very dark sea green (DMC 3812)
  - Dark lavender blue (DMC 3838)

Instructions

1 With the white pencil, draw the centerlines on the fabric in both horizontal and vertical directions. Draw the 4" x 8" (10.2 x 20.3cm) brick outline. Draw the cutting lines using the template provided on page 112. If your brick is a different size, adjust the template and all dimensions to fit the size needed.

2 Print or photocopy the template on the sheet of Sticky Fabri-Solvy stabilizer. With the water-soluble pencil, draw the centerlines on the fabric in both horizontal and vertical directions. Remove the backing paper from the stabilizer sheet. Align the centerlines of the template with the white pencil lines. Gently press the adhesive side of the stabilizer sheet onto the fabric. Use a few straight pins to hold the stabilizer sheet firmly in place.

3 Insert the fabric into the hoop. Stitch the elements in the following sequence.
   1. Text
   2. Border

4 Cut the fabric along the cutting lines drawn in step 1. This will leave excess fabric to wrap all six sides of the brick. Cut one of the fabric scraps slightly smaller than 4" x 8" (10.2 x 20.3cm). This will be used for the bottom of the brick and applied in step 6. Wrap the brick in plastic wrap.

5 Gently rinse the fabric under running water to remove the stabilizer. Dry flat on a clean surface, such as a paper towel. After the fabric is dry, press it with a warm iron.

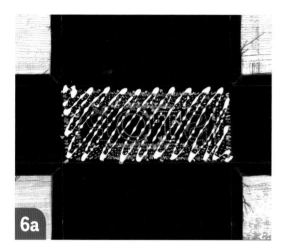

6a

6 Lay the fabric face down on a smooth working surface. Apply white glue evenly to the backside of the stitched fabric. Wrap the excess fabric on all four sides onto the backside of the brick. Apply white glue to a separate piece of fabric, and then apply it to the bottom of the brick with even pressure. Allow it to dry.

6b

6c

Color Diagram

Copy at 250%

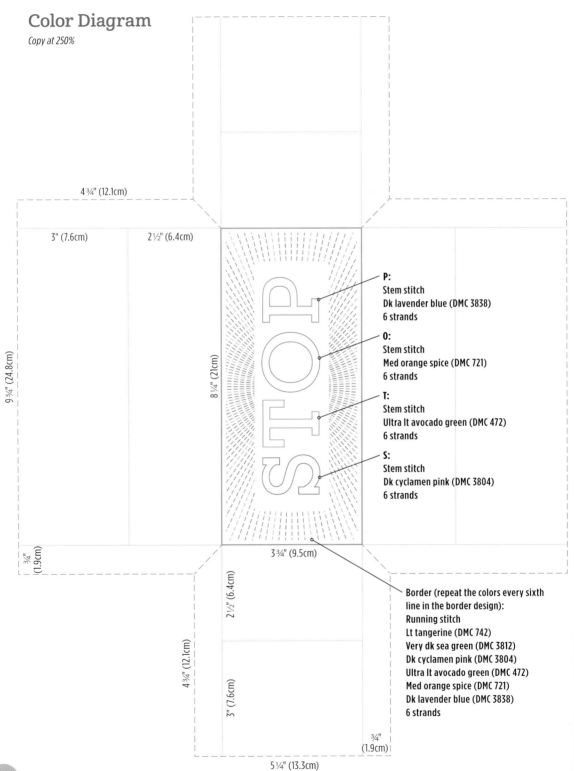

4 ¾" (12.1cm)

3" (7.6cm)   2 ½" (6.4cm)

9 ¾" (24.8cm)

8 ¼" (21cm)

P:
Stem stitch
Dk lavender blue (DMC 3838)
6 strands

O:
Stem stitch
Med orange spice (DMC 721)
6 strands

T:
Stem stitch
Ultra lt avocado green (DMC 472)
6 strands

S:
Stem stitch
Dk cyclamen pink (DMC 3804)
6 strands

¾"
(1.9cm)

3 ¾" (9.5cm)

2 ½" (6.4cm)

4 ¾" (12.1cm)

3" (7.6cm)

**Border (repeat the colors every sixth
line in the border design):**
Running stitch
Lt tangerine (DMC 742)
Very dk sea green (DMC 3812)
Dk cyclamen pink (DMC 3804)
Ultra lt avocado green (DMC 472)
Med orange spice (DMC 721)
Dk lavender blue (DMC 3838)
6 strands

¾"
(1.9cm)

5 ¼" (13.3cm)

ALTERNATE
DESIGNS
Copy at 400%

Top to Bottom Bath Towel

For those who reuse their towels (and shouldn't we all?), this is a great way to distinguish the top from the bottom. It's not just good for the environment to reuse a towel a few times, but it's also better for your utility bill. The less dirty laundry you go through, the less electricity you'll use. This is a quick and easy project for beginner and advanced embroiderers. Choose floss colors to coordinate with your bathroom color scheme or décor. For the text, copy and print the color diagram from this project. Alternate designs are also available on page 117.

Finished size: 30" x 54" (76.2 x 137.2cm) | Color diagram: page 117

Materials:

- 30" x 54" (75.2 x 137.2cm), 30" x 60" (75.2 x 152.4cm), or similar-size bath towel, white/color of your choice
- 8" (20.3cm) round embroidery hoop
- Sticky Fabri-Solvy stabilizer, one letter-size sheet
- Water-soluble pen (blue)
- Embroidery needle, size 2 to 4 (as preferred)
- Embroidery floss (one skein each), as listed, or modify to match bath towel:
  - Light peach (DMC 967)
  - Medium melon (DMC 3706)

Instructions

1 Print or photocopy two templates together on the sheet of Sticky Fabri-Solvy stabilizer. Cut the templates into two separate pieces with scissors. With the water-soluble pen, draw the centerline near the end of the towel in the vertical direction. Draw a horizontal line approximately 1" (2.5cm) above the woven band or hemline of the towel. (This position may vary depending on the size of the towels.) Remove the backing paper from one stabilizer piece. Align the centerlines of the template with the pen lines. Gently press the adhesive side of stabilizer piece onto the towel. Use a few straight pins to hold the stabilizer piece firmly in place. Repeat the same process with the remaining stabilizer piece at the other end of the towel.

2 Insert the one end of the towel into the hoop. Stitch the elements in the following sequence.
    1. Text, running stitch
    2. Text, whipped running stitch
    Repeat the same process with the other end of the towel.

3 Gently rinse each end of the towel under running water to remove the stabilizer. Dry flat on a clean surface, such as a paper towel. You may choose to throw the towel into a load of laundry to remove the stabilizer.

Color Diagram *Copy at 180%*

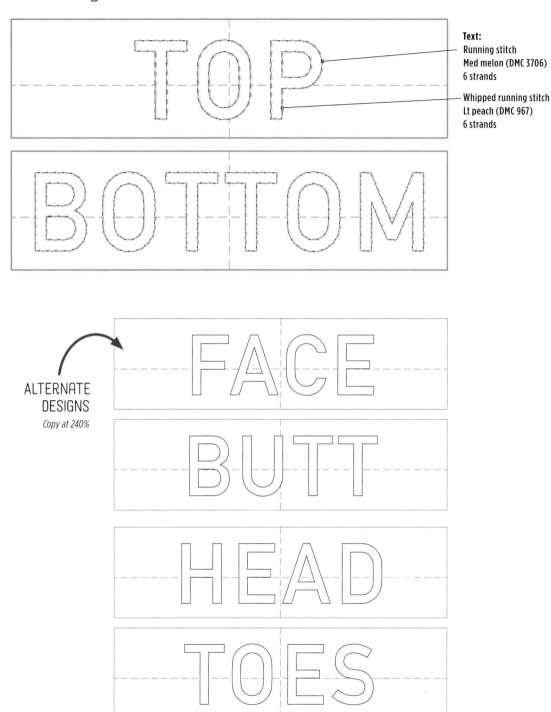

Text:
Running stitch
Med melon (DMC 3706)
6 strands

Whipped running stitch
Lt peach (DMC 967)
6 strands

ALTERNATE
DESIGNS
Copy at 240%

Four Eyed and Fabulous Eyeglass Case

This sassy design for reading glasses is fun and fashionable, featuring a leopard-print cat eye silhouette. The felt fabric provides a soft interior for glasses without a lining and is very simple to make. In the template section, choose from several options for the text. For larger-frame glasses, choose the alternate cutting lines on the color diagram. For the text, copy and print the color diagram from this project. An alternate design is also available on page 121.

Finished size: 2¾" x 7" (7 x 17.8cm) | Color diagram: page 121

Materials

- 10" x 10" (25.4 x 25.4cm) black felt
- 6" (15.2cm) round embroidery hoop
- Sticky Fabri-Solvy stabilizer, one letter-size sheet
- Water-soluble marking pencil (white)
- Embroidery needle, size 2 to 4 (as preferred)
- Embroidery floss (one skein each):
  - Ecru (DMC Ecru)
  - Dark hazelnut brown (DMC 420)
  - Light hazelnut brown (DMC 422)
  - Medium cranberry (DMC 602)

Instructions

1 Print or photocopy the template on the Sticky Fabri-Solvy stabilizer sheet. With the water-soluble pencil, draw the centerlines on the fabric in both horizontal and vertical directions. Remove the backing paper from the stabilizer sheet. Next, align the centerlines of the template with the white pencil lines. Gently press the adhesive side of the stabilizer sheet onto the fabric. Use a few straight pins to hold the stabilizer sheet firmly in place.

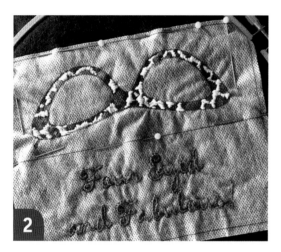

2 Insert the fabric into the hoop. Stitch the elements in the following sequence.
   1. Three colors of leopard-print fill
   2. Outline of the eyeglass shape
   3. Text

3 Cut the fabric along the cutting lines of the template. Gently rinse the eyeglass case under running water to remove the stabilizer. Dry flat on a clean surface, such as a paper towel. After the fabric is dry, press it with a warm iron.

4 Fold the eyeglass case in half with the right side and stitching facing out. Using a blanket stitch, sew along the open side and bottom end to seam both layers of fabric together. Ending with a knot, tuck the tail of floss inside the eyeglass case.

Color Diagram *Copy at 150%*

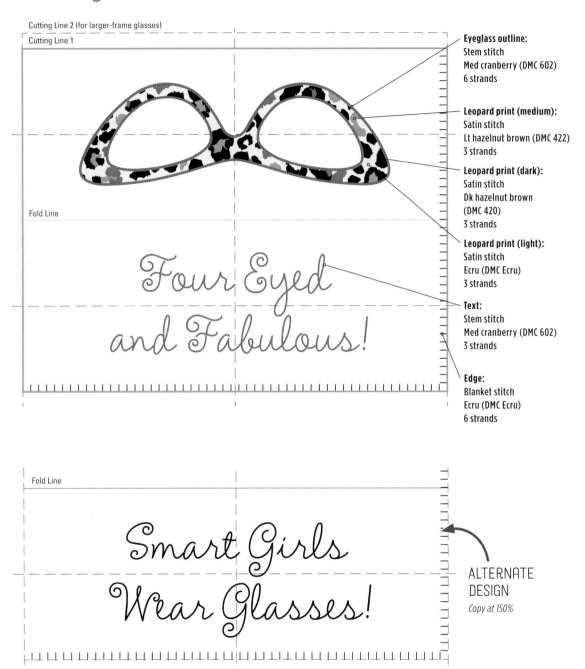

Cutting Line 2 (for larger-frame glasses)

Cutting Line 1

Fold Line

Eyeglass outline:
Stem stitch
Med cranberry (DMC 602)
6 strands

Leopard print (medium):
Satin stitch
Lt hazelnut brown (DMC 422)
3 strands

Leopard print (dark):
Satin stitch
Dk hazelnut brown
(DMC 420)
3 strands

Leopard print (light):
Satin stitch
Ecru (DMC Ecru)
3 strands

Text:
Stem stitch
Med cranberry (DMC 602)
3 strands

Edge:
Blanket stitch
Ecru (DMC Ecru)
6 strands

Four Eyed and Fabulous!

Fold Line

Smart Girls Wear Glasses!

ALTERNATE
DESIGN
Copy at 150%

Hello Gorgeous Cosmetic Bag

Say "Hello, gorgeous" to this pretty cosmetic bag. With sweet words of beauty affirmation, this makeup bag is the perfect way to keep all your cosmetics organized. Take a plain cosmetic bag and dress it up with a stitched phrase and border. For yourself, stash it in your purse for glamour on the go. It makes a useful and appreciated gift filled with goodies. As a bridesmaid gift, your bridal party can use the bag to hold the products needed on that special day. For the text, copy and print the color diagram from this project. Alternate designs are also available on page 125.

Finished size: 8" x 11" (20.3 x 28cm) or similar-size cosmetic bag
Color diagram: page 125

Materials

- 8" x 11" (20.3 x 28cm) or similar-size fabric cosmetic bag (canvas or nylon)
- 6" (15.2 cm) round embroidery hoop
- Sticky Fabri-Solvy stabilizer, one letter-size sheet
- Water-soluble pen (blue)
- Seam ripper (optional)
- Sewing thread color to match the lining color
- Embroidery needle, size 2 to 4 (as preferred)
- Embroidery floss (one skein each):
    - Very light ash gray (DMC 535)
    - Pale pumpkin (DMC 3825)

Instructions

1 If the cosmetic bag is lined, use a seam ripper to carefully remove the seam of the lining from the front of the bag. This will allow you to stitch on the front of the bag without stitching through the lining. If the bag is unlined, proceed to the next step.

2 Print or photocopy the template on the sheet of Sticky Fabri-Solvy stabilizer. With the water-soluble pen, draw the centerlines on the front of the cosmetic bag in both horizontal and vertical directions. Remove the backing paper from the stabilizer sheet. Align the centerlines of the template with the blue pen lines. Gently press the adhesive side of the stabilizer sheet onto the cosmetic bag. Use a few straight pins to hold the stabilizer sheet firmly in place.

3 Insert the fabric into the hoop. Stitch the elements in the following sequence.
1. Text outline
2. Text fill
3. Border

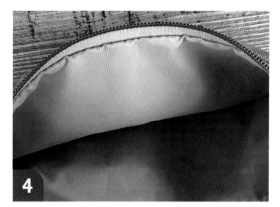

4 Gently rinse the cosmetic bag under running water to remove the stabilizer. Dry flat on a clean surface, such as a paper towel. After the fabric is dry, press it with a warm iron. Using a sewing thread color to match the lining color, sew the lining and bag together.

Color Diagram *Copy at 200%*

Text outline:
Stem stitch
Very lt ash gray
(DMC 535)
3 strands

Text fill:
Seed stitch
Pale pumpkin
(DMC 3825)
3 strands

Border (color 1):
Sheath stitch
Pale pumpkin
(DMC 3825)
3 strands

Border (color 2):
Sheath stitch
Very lt ash gray
(DMC 535)
3 strands

ALTERNATE
DESIGNS
Copy at 400%

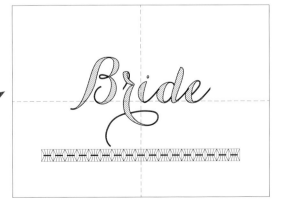

Bookworm Fabric Bookmarks

These witty bookmarks make great gifts for readers and anyone using hardcover novels, textbooks, and cookbooks. Mix and match scraps of quilt cotton fabric with coordinating ribbon and floss colors. For the text, copy and print the color diagram from this project. Alternate designs are also available on page 129.

Finished size: 2½" x 7½" (6.4 x 19cm) | Color diagram: page 129

Materials

- 7" x 8½" (17.8 x 21.6cm) scraps of quilt cotton (one piece per bookmark)
- 3" x 8" (7.6 x 20.3cm) fusible interfacing or iron-on adhesive sheet for fabric
- Two ⅜" x 5" (1 x 12.7cm) grosgrain ribbons (in coordinating colors per bookmark)
- Sticky Fabri-Solvy stabilizer, one letter-size sheet (yields 4 bookmarks)
- Water-soluble pen (blue)
- Embroidery needle, size 2 to 4 (as preferred)
- Embroidery floss (one skein each):
    - Dark lavender (DMC 209)
    - Black (DMC 310)
    - Dark lavender blue (DMC 3838)
    - Medium lavender blue (DMC 3839)

Instructions

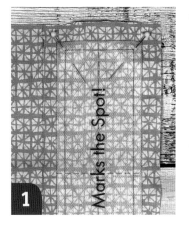

1 Print or photocopy the template on the sheet of Sticky Fabri-Solvy stabilizer. Up to three bookmarks will fit on one sheet. Cut the templates into separate pieces with scissors, leaving an extra margin outside the final cutting lines.

With the water-soluble pen, draw the centerlines on one piece of quilt fabric in both horizontal and vertical directions. Remove the backing paper from the sheet of the stabilizer. Align the centerlines of the template on the lower half of the fabric with the pen lines. Gently press the adhesive side of stabilizer piece onto the fabric. Use a few straight pins to hold each stabilizer piece firmly in place. Insert the fabric into the hoop.

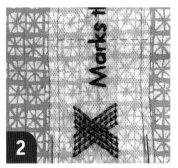

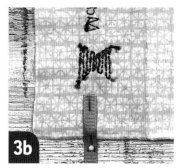

2 Stitch the elements in the following sequence.
   1. Text
   2. Icons

IMPORTANT NOTE:
DO NOT STITCH THE BORDERS UNTIL STEP 3.

3 Iron the fusible interfacing or adhesive to the backside and lower half of the bookmark. Remove the backing paper. Place the ribbon centered on the top end of the bookmark (the embroidered side), leaving the ribbon 4" (10.2cm) exposed and 1" (2.5cm) tucked inside the fabric. Use a straight pin close to the top edge to hold it in place. Fold the bookmark in half with the right sides facing out. Using a warm iron, press hard to create a strong bond between the two layers of fabric.

4 Stitch the border through both layers of the fabric. Cut both layers of the fabric along the cutting lines of the template, avoiding the ribbon.

5 Gently rinse the bookmark under running water to remove the stabilizer. Dry flat on a clean surface, such as a paper towel. After the fabric is dry, press it with a warm iron.

Color Diagram *Copy at 180%*

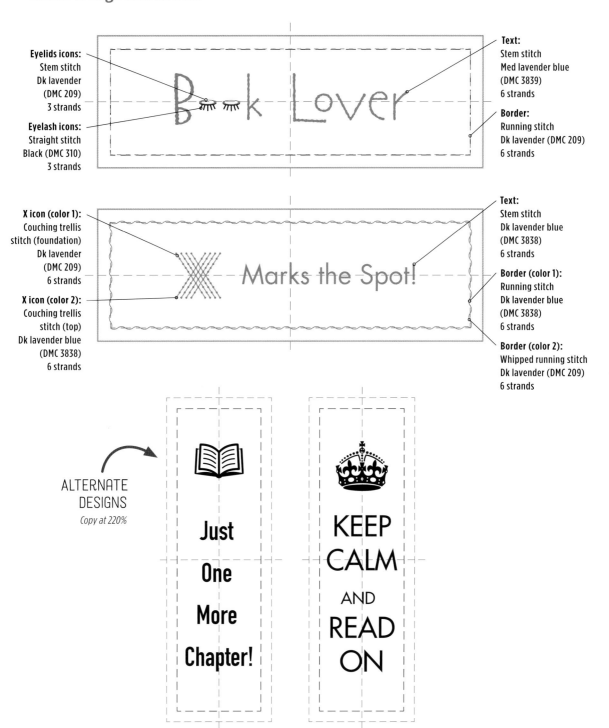

Eyelids icons:
Stem stitch
Dk lavender
(DMC 209)
3 strands

Eyelash icons:
Straight stitch
Black (DMC 310)
3 strands

Text:
Stem stitch
Med lavender blue
(DMC 3839)
6 strands

Border:
Running stitch
Dk lavender (DMC 209)
6 strands

X icon (color 1):
Couching trellis
stitch (foundation)
Dk lavender
(DMC 209)
6 strands

X icon (color 2):
Couching trellis
stitch (top)
Dk lavender blue
(DMC 3838)
6 strands

Text:
Stem stitch
Dk lavender blue
(DMC 3838)
6 strands

Border (color 1):
Running stitch
Dk lavender blue
(DMC 3838)
6 strands

Border (color 2):
Whipped running stitch
Dk lavender (DMC 209)
6 strands

ALTERNATE
DESIGNS
Copy at 220%

Just

One

More

Chapter!

KEEP
CALM
AND
READ
ON

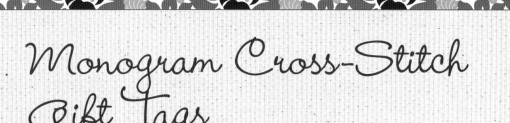

Monogram Cross-Stitch Gift Tags

Complete the look of your gifts for loved ones with unique personalized gift tags, featuring a heart with a monogram. Your recipients will be delighted by your attention to detail and chic gifting style. The gift tags are reusable many times over and appropriate for all occasions, including birthdays, graduations, holidays, and more. The basic cross-stitch design is a good beginner project or a quick and easy project for an advanced embroiderer. Copy and print the alphabet from page 168 for this project.

Finished size: 3¾" x 7½" (9.5 x 19.1cm) | Color diagram: page 133

Materials:

- Two 5" x 10" (12.7 x 25.4cm) pieces of gray felt
- 4" x 8" (10.2 x 20.3cm) waste canvas (14-count package)
- 4" x 8" (10.2 x 20.3cm) fusible interfacing or iron-on adhesive sheet
- Water-soluble pen (blue)
- Single-hole puncher (typically used for paper)
- ⅛" wide x 18" long (0.3 x 45.7cm) ribbon in coordinating color
- Embroidery needle, size 2 to 4 (as preferred)

- Embroidery floss (one skein each):
  - Red (DMC 321)
  - Very light ash gray (DMC 535)
  - Violet (DMC 553)
  - Medium cranberry (DMC 602)
  - Bright chartreuse (DMC 704)
  - Medium tangerine (DMC 741)
  - Medium yellow (DMC 743)
  - Medium pink (DMC 776)
  - Light baby blue (DMC 3325)
  - Dark bright turquoise (DMC 3844)

Instructions

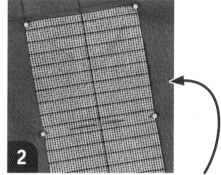

1 With the water-soluble pen, draw the centerlines on the fabric in both horizontal and vertical directions. Draw the outline of the gift tag by referring to the template provided on page 133. It should measure 3¾" x 7½" (9.5 x 19.1cm).

2 Center the waste canvas on felt fabric and secure it in place with straight pins.

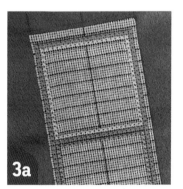

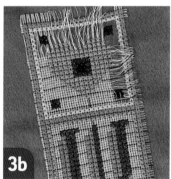

3 Using the 14-count grid of the waste canvas as your guide, stitch the cross-stitches by skipping every other hole to yield 7 stitches per inch (few centimeters). Refer to the color diagram to count your stitches. Stitch the elements in the following sequence.

   1. Borders   2. Heart   3. Squares   4. Text

After all the stitching is complete, carefully pull out all the threads of the waste canvas. This must be done one thread at a time in order to not disturb the stitching. Take your time, as this process takes a bit of patience.

4 Iron the fusible interfacing or adhesive to the backside of the gift tag. Remove the backing paper from the interfacing. Place the blank piece of felt fabric to the backside of the gift tag with the right sides facing out. Using a warm iron, press firmly to create a strong bond between the two layers of fabric.

5a

5b

5 Cut both layers of the felt fabric along the cutting lines of the template. Mark a center point at the top of the gift tag. Using the hole puncher, punch a hole through both layers of felt. Stitch around the hole through both layers of the fabric with a blanket stitch. Working by eye, make 12 stitches in a circle following the sequence of numbers on a clock face. Thread the ribbon through the reinforced hole.

Color Diagram *Copy at 200%*

SEE FULL
ALPHABET SET
ON PAGE 168

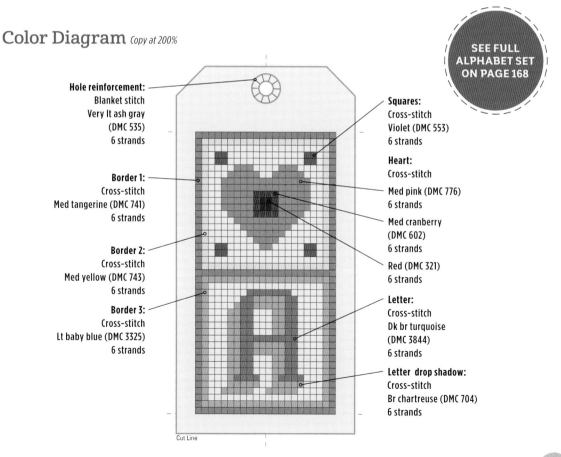

Hole reinforcement:
Blanket stitch
Very lt ash gray
(DMC 535)
6 strands

Border 1:
Cross-stitch
Med tangerine (DMC 741)
6 strands

Border 2:
Cross-stitch
Med yellow (DMC 743)
6 strands

Border 3:
Cross-stitch
Lt baby blue (DMC 3325)
6 strands

Squares:
Cross-stitch
Violet (DMC 553)
6 strands

Heart:
Cross-stitch
Med pink (DMC 776)
6 strands

Med cranberry
(DMC 602)
6 strands

Red (DMC 321)
6 strands

Letter:
Cross-stitch
Dk br turquoise
(DMC 3844)
6 strands

Letter drop shadow:
Cross-stitch
Br chartreuse (DMC 704)
6 strands

Cut Line

Reduce, Recycle, Reuse Tote Bag

This tote bag is great for carrying around stuff at school, work, or when shopping. Most importantly, it promotes the use of reusable bags and encourages eco-friendly habits. Make the appliqué, then apply it to a plain bag you already own or purchase plain canvas bags in bulk online. These bags make great gifts, and the materials are low in cost. Use scraps of quilt fabric on hand or buy a fat quarter, choosing from dozens of print options. For the text, copy and print the color diagram from this project. Alternate designs are also available on page 139.

Finished sizes: Tote bag—16" x 16" (40.6 x 40.6cm),
Appliqué—8" x 8" (20.3 x 20.3cm) | Color diagram: page 138

Materials:

- 16" x 16" (40.6 x 40.6cm) fabric tote bag (or size of your choice)
- 8" (20.3cm) round embroidery hoop
- Sticky Fabri-Solvy stabilizer, one letter-size sheet
- Water-soluble pen (blue)
- 12" x 12" (30.5 x 30.5cm) quilt cotton (color and design of your choice)
- Embroidery needle, size 2 to 4 (as preferred)

- Embroidery floss, as listed, or modify to match quilt fabrics (one skein each):
  - Dark lavender (DMC 209)
  - Violet (DMC 553)
  - Dark cranberry (DMC 601)
  - Bright green (DMC 700)
  - Chartreuse (DMC 703)
  - Medium orange spice (DMC 721)
  - Light sea green (DMC 964)
  - Medium melon (DMC 3706)
  - Pale pumpkin (DMC 3825)
  - Dark bright turquoise (DMC 3844)
  - Medium bright turquoise (DMC 3845)

Instructions

1 Print or photocopy the template on the sheet of Sticky Fabri-Solvy stabilizer. With the water-soluble pen, draw the centerlines on the quilt fabric in both horizontal and vertical directions. Remove the backing paper from the stabilizer sheet. Align the centerlines of the template with the pen lines. Gently press the adhesive side of the stabilizer sheet onto the fabric. Use a few straight pins to hold the stabilizer sheet firmly in place.

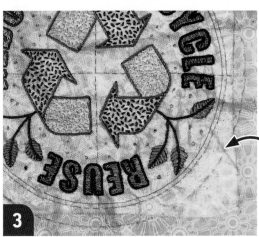

2 Insert the fabric into the hoop. Stitch the elements in the following sequence.
   1. Arrow icon outline
   2. Text outline
   3. Arrow icon fill
   4. Text fill
   5. Stems
   6. Leaves

3 With the water-soluble pen, draw a 1" (2.5cm) seam allowance outside the 8" (20.3cm) circle template. Cut the fabric along the new pen line.

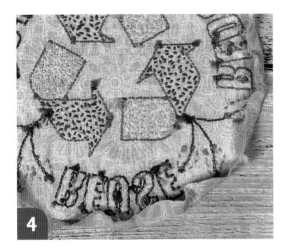

4 Gently rinse the fabric under running water to remove the stabilizer. Dry flat on a clean surface, such as a paper towel. After the fabric is dry, press it with a warm iron. Fold the 1" (2.5cm) seam allowance and press with a warm iron to form the finished 8" (20.3cm) circular appliqué.

5 With the water-soluble pen, draw the centerlines on the tote bag in both horizontal and vertical directions. Center the appliqué on the tote bag. Align the centerlines of the appliqué with the pen lines on the tote bag. Use a few straight pins to hold the appliqué firmly in place.

6 Stitch around the appliqué with a blanket stitch going through both layers of the quilt fabric and tote bag for a sturdy finished edge.

Color Diagram *Copy at 170%*

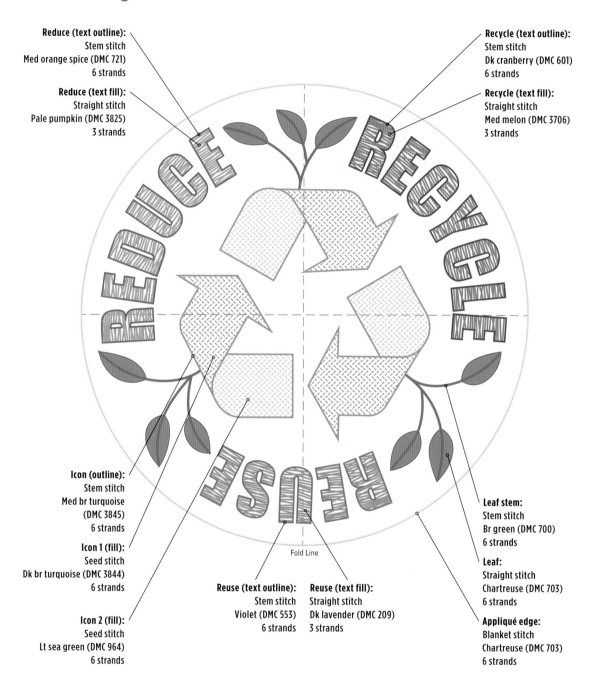

Reduce (text outline):
Stem stitch
Med orange spice (DMC 721)
6 strands

Reduce (text fill):
Straight stitch
Pale pumpkin (DMC 3825)
3 strands

Recycle (text outline):
Stem stitch
Dk cranberry (DMC 601)
6 strands

Recycle (text fill):
Straight stitch
Med melon (DMC 3706)
3 strands

Icon (outline):
Stem stitch
Med br turquoise
(DMC 3845)
6 strands

Icon 1 (fill):
Seed stitch
Dk br turquoise (DMC 3844)
6 strands

Icon 2 (fill):
Seed stitch
Lt sea green (DMC 964)
6 strands

Fold Line

Reuse (text outline):
Stem stitch
Violet (DMC 553)
6 strands

Reuse (text fill):
Straight stitch
Dk lavender (DMC 209)
3 strands

Leaf stem:
Stem stitch
Br green (DMC 700)
6 strands

Leaf:
Straight stitch
Chartreuse (DMC 703)
6 strands

Appliqué edge:
Blanket stitch
Chartreuse (DMC 703)
6 strands

ALTERNATE DESIGNS
Copy at 220%

Fold Line

Fold Line

Reduce, Recycle, Reuse Tote Bag

Get Organized Canvas Pouches

These little pouches have a hundred and one uses, and they can be useful to any member of the family. The small pouch can be used for extra cash and coins. The larger pouch can be used to hold all those small things that get lost in a purse, backpack, or tote bag, from lipstick and mints to pens and phone cords. Look for blank pouches where cosmetic bags or pencil cases are sold. They can be purchased in sets or bulk online in a variety of sizes. For the text, copy and print the color diagram from this project. Alternate designs are also available on page 143.

Finished sizes: Small pouch—3" x 8" (7.6 x 20.3cm),
Large pouch—4½" x 7½" (11.4 x 17.8cm) | Color diagram: page 143

Materials:

- 3" x 8" (7.6 x 20.3cm) canvas or nylon unlined fabric pouch
- Unlined fabric pouch (canvas or nylon), medium size, 4½" x 7½" (11.4 x 17.8cm)
- 6" (15.2cm) round embroidery hoop
- Sticky Fabri-Solvy stabilizer, one letter-size sheet (yields 4 pouches)
- Water-soluble pen (blue)
- Embroidery needle, size 2 to 4 (as preferred)
- Embroidery floss (one skein each)
- Gradated color floss or solid color of your choice

Instructions

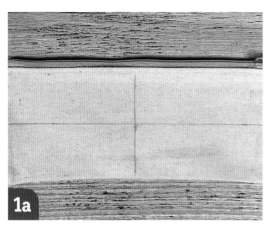

1 Print or photocopy the template on the sheet of Sticky Fabri-Solvy stabilizer. Up to four pouch templates will fit on one sheet. Cut the templates into separate pieces with scissors. With the water-soluble pen, draw the centerlines on the front of the pouch bag in both horizontal and vertical directions. Remove the backing paper from the stabilizer sheet. Align the centerlines of the template with the blue pen lines. Gently press the adhesive side of the stabilizer sheet onto the cosmetic bag. Use a few straight pins to hold the stabilizer sheet firmly in place. Repeat the same process with the remaining pouches.

2 Insert the fabric into the hoop, then stitch the text.

3 Gently rinse the pouch under running water to remove the stabilizer. Dry flat on a clean surface, such as a paper towel. After the fabric is dry, press it with a warm iron.

Color Diagram *Copy at 180%*

Text:
Stem stitch
Color floss
(your choice)
6 strands

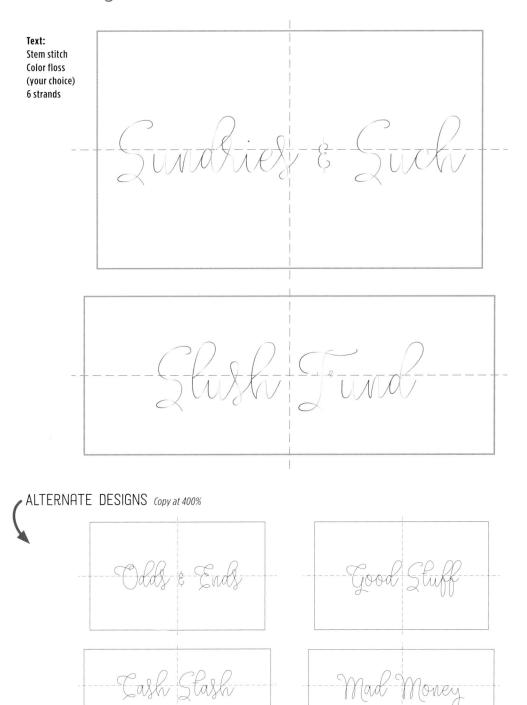

ALTERNATE DESIGNS *Copy at 400%*

Personalizing Name Labels (or Everything!)

Go crazy personalizing by stitching directly onto any fabric item you can get your hands on, with a name, nickname, or whimsical phrase. Instructions here are provided to stitch on a label that can then be attached to caps, garments, or home accessories. The label can be made from scraps of quilt fabric, twill ribbon, denim, or more. The options are endless. Copy and print the alphabet from page 169 for this project.

Finished size: varies | Color diagrams: pages 146 and 149

Materials:

- Sticky Fabri-Solvy stabilizer, one letter-size sheet
- Water-soluble pen (blue) for light fabrics, or water-soluble marking pencil (white) for dark fabrics
- Fine-point black felt pen (such as a fine-point Sharpie)
- Embroidery needle, size 2 to 4 (as preferred)

Option A

- Round embroidery hoop, 4" (10.2cm) diameter
- Embroidery floss (one skein), or color of your choice:
  - Black (DMC 310)

Option B

- 2" x 3½" (5.1 x 10.2cm) piece of scrap quilt cotton in color of your choice (adjust size for longer phrase), two pieces per label (one for the front and one for the back)
- Embroidery floss (one skein each), or color of your choice:
  - Black (DMC 310)
  - Chartreuse (DMC 703)
  - Light baby blue (DMC 3325)

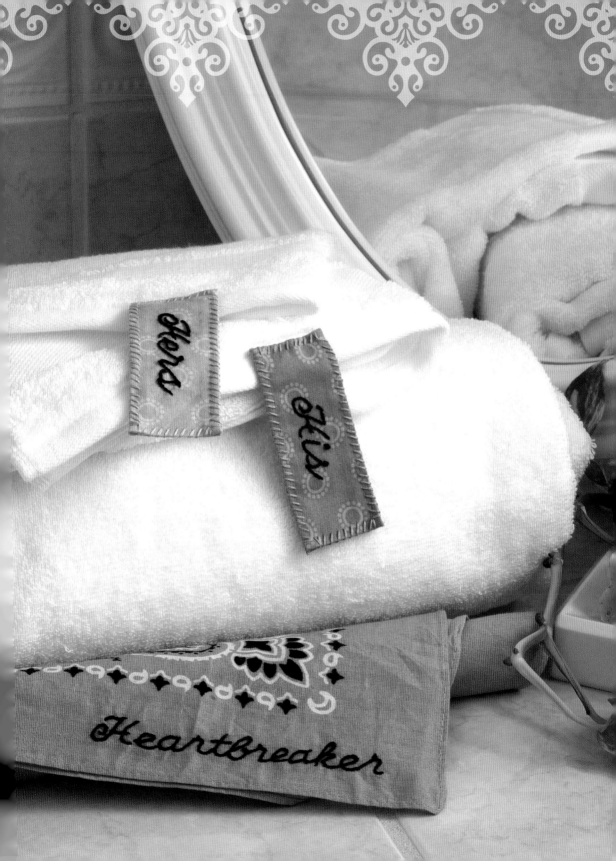

Instructions

  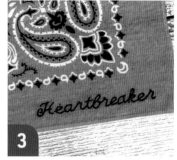

1 Draw straight lines on the sheet of Sticky Fabri-Solvy stabilizer to be used as a baseline for the text. Trace your name or phrase directly on the stabilizer to create the template. Carefully align all letters along the baseline, and pay attention to even spacing between letters. Cut the template with scissors, leaving an extra margin around the text. With the water-soluble pen, draw a horizontal line where you plan to place the embroidery on the item. Remove the backing paper from the stabilizer sheet. Align the baseline of the text template with the pen line. Gently press the adhesive side of the stabilizer sheet onto the fabric. Use a few straight pins to hold the stabilizer sheet firmly in place.

2 Insert the item into the hoop. Stitch the text.

3 Gently rinse the item under running water to remove the stabilizer. Dry flat on a clean surface, such as a paper towel. After the fabric is dry, press it with a warm iron.

Color Diagram *Copy at 100%*

Text (Heartbreaker):
Stem stitch
Black (DMC 310)
6 strands

Heartbreaker

Sophia

Text (Sophia):
Backstitch
Black (DMC 310)
3 strands

SEE FULL ALPHABET SET ON PAGE 169

Instructions

1 Draw straight lines on the sheet of Sticky Fabri-Solvy stabilizer to be used as a baseline for the text. Trace a name or phrase from the alphabet template directly onto the stabilizer to use as the stitching template. Carefully align all letters along the baseline and pay attention to even spacing between the letters for a neat, finished result. Cut the template with scissors, leaving an extra

margin around the text. With the water-soluble pen, draw a horizontal line where you plan to place the embroidery on the label. Draw a centerline in the vertical direction. Remove the backing paper from the stabilizer piece. Align the baseline of the text template with the pen line. Gently press the adhesive side of the stabilizer piece onto the fabric. Use a few straight pins to hold the stabilizer piece firmly in place.

2 Stitch the text. No hoop is required for this project.

3 Gently rinse the item under running water to remove the stabilizer. Dry flat on a clean surface, such as a paper towel. After the fabric is dry, press it with a warm iron.

4 Draw the fold line around all four sides at ⅜" (9.5cm) from the trimmed edge of the stitched label. Fold along the line and press along the edges with a warm iron. Repeat the process on all four edges of the blank fabric piece for the back of the label. Pin the front and back labels together with the right sides facing out. With a glove stitch, sew around all four edges. With a blind stitch, sew the name label to the item, attaching one end as a hanging tag, or on all four edges as a flat label.

Color Diagram *Copy at 100%*

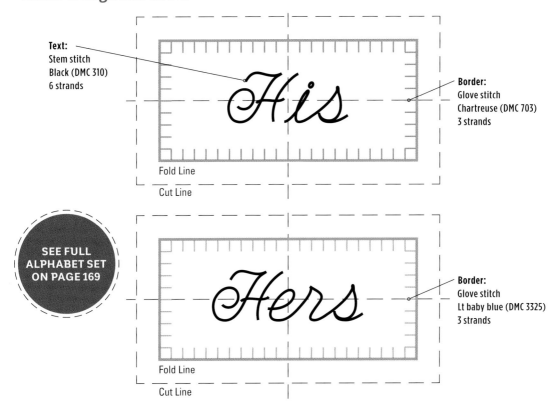

Text:
Stem stitch
Black (DMC 310)
6 strands

Border:
Glove stitch
Chartreuse (DMC 703)
3 strands

Fold Line

Cut Line

SEE FULL
ALPHABET SET
ON PAGE 169

Border:
Glove stitch
Lt baby blue (DMC 3325)
3 strands

Fold Line

Cut Line

Airport Code Luggage Tags

An aviation- and travel-inspired luggage tag, featuring international airport codes, is a certain way to make luggage stand out at the baggage claim. The tags are a nice way to dress up a backpack or tote bag and assure identification at all times. This is a quick and easy project for beginner and advanced stitchers. Make up your own combination of letters from the alphabet provided on page 172. Alternate designs are also available on page 153. Look up any international airport code at *www.airportcodes.org*.

Finished size: 3" x 5½" (7.6 x 14cm) | Color diagram: page 153

Materials:

- 8" x 8" (20.3 x 20.3cm) pink felt (or color of your choice)
- Sticky Fabri-Solvy stabilizer, one letter-size sheet
- Water-soluble pen (blue)
- Single-hole puncher (typically used for paper)

- ⅜" wide x 18" long (1 x 45.7cm) ribbon in coordinating color
- Embroidery needle, size 2 to 4 (as preferred)
- Embroidery floss (one skein each):
  - Plum (DMC 718)
  - Dark orange spice (DMC 720)
  - Medium yellow green (DMC 3347)
  - Very dark straw (DMC 3852)

Instructions

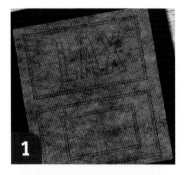

1 Print or photocopy both front and back templates on the sheet of Sticky Fabri-Solvy stabilizer. With the water-soluble pen, draw the centerlines on fabric in both horizontal and vertical directions. Remove the backing paper from the sheet of the stabilizer. Align the centerlines of the template with the pen lines. Gently press the adhesive side of the stabilizer piece onto the fabric. Cut the piece in half to separate the front and back templates. Use a few straight pins to hold each stabilizer piece firmly in place.

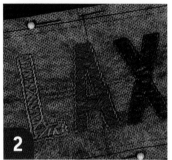

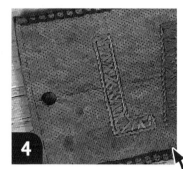

2 Insert the fabric for the front of the luggage tag into the hoop. Stitch the elements in the following sequence.
   1. Text outline
   2. Text fill

IMPORTANT NOTE: DO NOT STITCH THE BORDERS UNTIL STEP 5.

3 For the back of the luggage tag, use scissors to remove the center window area. Using a blanket stitch, and then stitch around the window edge.

4 Trim both the front and back luggage tags along the cutting lines of the template. Pin the front and back luggage tags together with the right sides facing out. Using the hole puncher, make a hole through both layers of felt fabric. Using a blanket stitch, stitch around the outer three edges. Leave an open end where the hole is located.

5 Gently rinse the luggage tags under running water to remove the stabilizer. Dry flat on a clean surface, such as a paper towel. After the fabric is dry, press it with a warm iron.

6 You may photocopy the information card from the book and fill in the form. Laminate if desired. Trim to size along the cutting lines, and insert the name information card inside the open end of the luggage tag. Thread the ribbon through the hole.

Color Diagram *Copy at 150%*

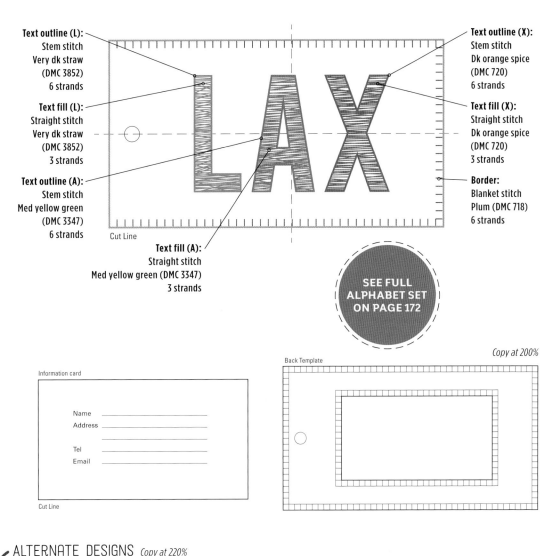

Text outline (L):
Stem stitch
Very dk straw
(DMC 3852)
6 strands

Text fill (L):
Straight stitch
Very dk straw
(DMC 3852)
3 strands

Text outline (A):
Stem stitch
Med yellow green
(DMC 3347)
6 strands

Cut Line

Text fill (A):
Straight stitch
Med yellow green (DMC 3347)
3 strands

Text outline (X):
Stem stitch
Dk orange spice
(DMC 720)
6 strands

Text fill (X):
Straight stitch
Dk orange spice
(DMC 720)
3 strands

Border:
Blanket stitch
Plum (DMC 718)
6 strands

SEE FULL ALPHABET SET ON PAGE 172

Information card

Name
Address

Tel
Email

Cut Line

Back Template

Copy at 200%

ALTERNATE DESIGNS *Copy at 220%*

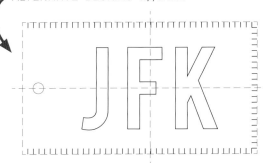

Geometric Monogram Tennis Shoes

A monogram with playful geometric shapes is a great way to dress up basic canvas sneakers. Use a first name initial on one shoe and a last name initial on the other show. Copy and print the alphabets from pages 170 and 171 for this project.

Finished size of stitched design: 2¾" x 6" (7 x 15.2cm) | **Color diagram: page 157**

Materials

- Canvas fabric tennis shoes
  (in your choice of color)
- Sticky Fabri-Solvy stabilizer, one letter-size sheet
- Water-soluble pen (blue)
- Tracing paper, one sheet
- Fine-point felt pen (black)
- Embroidery needle, size 2 to 4 (as preferred)
- Embroidery floss (1 skein each):
  - Lime green (DMC 166)
  - Violet (DMC 327)
  - Coral (DMC 351)
  - Dark Wedgewood (DMC 517)
  - Dark cranberry (DMC 601)
  - Light straw (DMC 3822)

Instructions

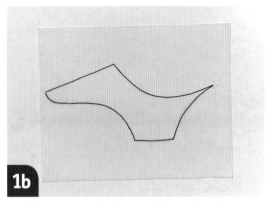

1 Print or photocopy two templates on the sheet of Sticky Fabri-Solvy stabilizer. Cut the templates into two separate pieces with scissors, leaving an extra margin outside the final cutting lines. Trace the side panels of both shoes onto tracing paper with a thin black pen. Lay the template printed on stabilizer over the tracing and make any adjustments to the cutting lines needed to fit your specific pair of shoes. As shoes vary in size and shape, you may need to adjust the placement of the design to fit your shoes nicely. Cut the template in the shape of the shoe side panels. Remove backing paper from the stabilizer sheet. Gently press the adhesive side of the stabilizer sheet onto the shoes. Use a few straight pins to hold the stabilizer sheet firmly in place.

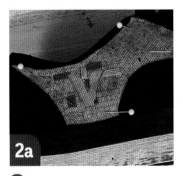

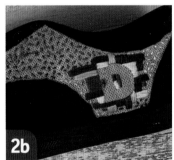

2 No hoop is needed for this project. Stitch the elements in the following sequence.
1. Geometric shapes
2. Random lines

3 Gently rinse the shoes under running water to remove the stabilizer. Dry flat on a clean surface, such as a paper towel.

Color Diagram
Copy at 100%

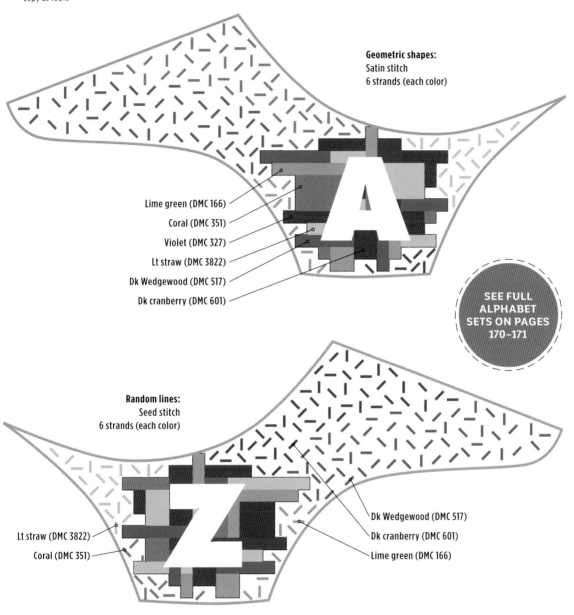

Geometric shapes:
Satin stitch
6 strands (each color)

Lime green (DMC 166)
Coral (DMC 351)
Violet (DMC 327)
Lt straw (DMC 3822)
Dk Wedgewood (DMC 517)
Dk cranberry (DMC 601)

SEE FULL
ALPHABET
SETS ON PAGES
170–171

Random lines:
Seed stitch
6 strands (each color)

Lt straw (DMC 3822)
Coral (DMC 351)

Dk Wedgewood (DMC 517)
Dk cranberry (DMC 601)
Lime green (DMC 166)

Wild and Free Shirt

Dress up a casual or dressy button-down shirt with a hand-stitched phrase on the pocket to really make a statement. Embroidery adds a nice textured look to an otherwise plain garment. Consider adding beads or buttons to embellish the designs. This is a very quick project to make for any skill level. For the text, copy and print the color diagram from this project. Alternate designs are also available on page 161.

Finished size of pocket: 3¾" x 4¼" (9.5 x 10.8cm) | Color diagram: page 161

Materials:

- Button-down shirt with pocket, 4" x 4½" (10.2 x 11.4cm) minimum pocket size
- Sticky Fabri-Solvy stabilizer, one letter-size sheet
- Water-soluble pen (blue)
- Embroidery needle, size 2 to 4 (as preferred)
- Embroidery floss (one skein each):
  - Very dark blue violet (DMC 333)
  - Blue (DMC 336)
  - Dark Wedgewood (DMC 517)
  - Light blue (DMC 813)
  - Ultra very light turquoise (DMC 3808)
  - Medium lavender blue (DMC 3839)
  - Medium teal green (DMC 3848)

Instructions

1 Print or photocopy the template on the sheet of Sticky Fabri-Solvy stabilizer. Trim the template into two pieces along the cutting lines with scissors. This will yield one template for the pocket and one template for the shirt chest area above the pocket. With the water-soluble pen, draw the centerlines on the shirt pocket in both horizontal and vertical directions. Remove the backing paper from the stabilizer piece. Align the centerlines of the template with the pen lines. Gently press the adhesive side of the stabilizer piece onto the pocket. Use a few straight pins to hold each stabilizer piece firmly in place.

2 No hoop is required for this project. Use your fingers to hold the pocket tight while sewing through the pocket layer only, and avoid sewing through the shirt layer. Stitch the elements in the following sequence.
1. Text
2. Stems
3. Dots

3 Gently rinse the shirt pocket under running water to remove the stabilizer. Dry flat on a clean surface, such as a paper towel. After the fabric is dry, press it with a warm iron, taking care to not iron over the French knots.

Color Diagram

Copy at 150%

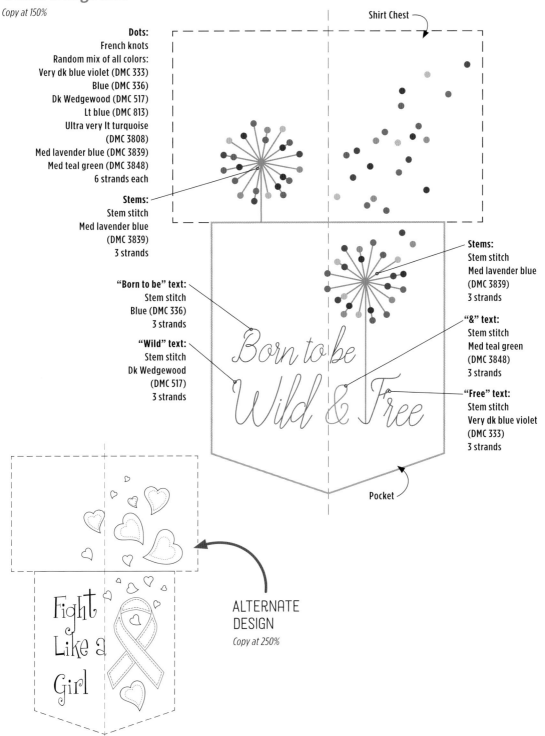

Dots:
French knots
Random mix of all colors:
Very dk blue violet (DMC 333)
Blue (DMC 336)
Dk Wedgewood (DMC 517)
Lt blue (DMC 813)
Ultra very lt turquoise (DMC 3808)
Med lavender blue (DMC 3839)
Med teal green (DMC 3848)
6 strands each

Stems:
Stem stitch
Med lavender blue (DMC 3839)
3 strands

"Born to be" text:
Stem stitch
Blue (DMC 336)
3 strands

"Wild" text:
Stem stitch
Dk Wedgewood (DMC 517)
3 strands

Shirt Chest

Stems:
Stem stitch
Med lavender blue (DMC 3839)
3 strands

"&" text:
Stem stitch
Med teal green (DMC 3848)
3 strands

"Free" text:
Stem stitch
Very dk blue violet (DMC 333)
3 strands

Pocket

Born to be Wild & Free

Fight Like a Girl

ALTERNATE DESIGN
Copy at 250%

Summer of Love Jeans Pocket

This fun 1960s-inspired design is the word "love" in a heart, shown here in two ways. This design may also be made as a separate patch and applied to a variety of garments, such as a jean jacket or backpack. Option A is a quick and easy version since it only requires stitching of the outline of the template. Use graduated color floss for a tie-dye look. Option B is more elaborate and takes more time to fully fill in the heart with stitches. Use up to 17 colors of floss for a fully gradated rainbow affect. Copy and print the color diagram from page 165.

Finished size: 3¼" x 4" (8.3 x 10.2cm) | Color diagram: page 165

Materials

- Pair of denim jeans with back pocket, 4" x 5" (10.2 x 12.7cm) minimum pocket size
- Sticky Fabri-Solvy stabilizer, one letter-size sheet
- Water-soluble pen (blue)
- Seam ripper
- Heavy-duty jeans thread (made especially for denim jeans by a variety of manufacturers; available in gold, white, or blue; choose the one that best matches your jeans
- Embroidery needle, size 2 to 4 (as preferred)

Option A
- Embroidery floss (one skein each):
  - Gradated color floss of your choice

Option B
- Embroidery floss (one skein each):
  - Bright green (DMC 165)
  - Lime green (DMC 166)
  - Red (DMC 321)
  - Very dark blue violet (DMC 333)
  - Medium cranberry (DMC 602)
  - Bright red (DMC 666)

- Bright green (DMC 700)
- Chartreuse (DMC 703)
- Medium orange spice (DMC 721)
- Very light topaz (DMC 727)
- Medium tangerine (DMC 741)
- Medium yellow (DMC 743)
- Medium pink (DMC 776)
- Light plum (DMC 3607)
- Dark lavender blue (DMC 3838)
- Medium lavender blue (DMC 3839)
- Light lavender blue (DMC 3840)

Instructions

1a

1b

1 Use a seam ripper to carefully remove the seam from one side of the pocket. This will allow you to stitch on the pocket more freely and avoid sewing through the pants layer. Print or photocopy the template on the sheet of Sticky Fabri-Solvy stabilizer. Trim the template along the cutting lines with scissors.

   With the water-soluble pen, draw the centerlines on the denim jeans pocket in both horizontal and vertical directions. Remove the backing paper from the stabilizer piece, then align the centerlines of the template with the pen lines. Gently press the adhesive side of the stabilizer piece onto the pocket. Use a few straight pins to hold each stabilizer piece firmly in place.

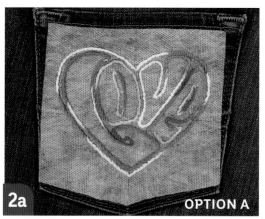

2a   OPTION A

2b   OPTION B

2 No hoop is required for this project. Stitch the outline for Option A or fill for Option B. Use your fingers to hold the pocket tight while sewing through the pocket layer only and avoid sewing through the pants layer.

3 Using the jeans thread, reattach the pocket back in place.

Color Diagram

Copy at 125%

Option A (outline version):
Stem stitch
6 strands (each color)

Option B (filled version):
Short and long stitch
6 strands (each color)

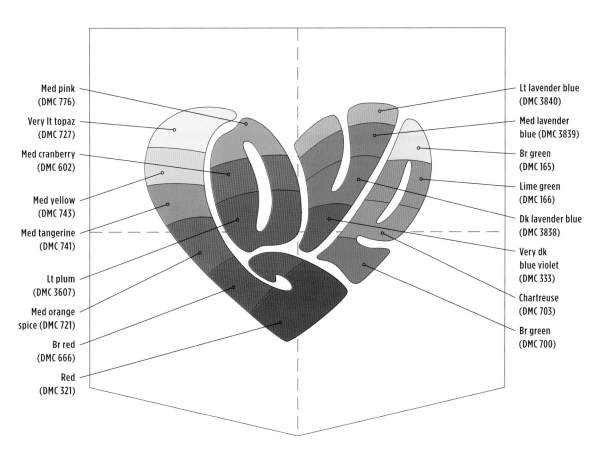

Med pink
(DMC 776)

Very lt topaz
(DMC 727)

Med cranberry
(DMC 602)

Med yellow
(DMC 743)

Med tangerine
(DMC 741)

Lt plum
(DMC 3607)

Med orange
spice (DMC 721)

Br red
(DMC 666)

Red
(DMC 321)

Lt lavender blue
(DMC 3840)

Med lavender
blue (DMC 3839)

Br green
(DMC 165)

Lime green
(DMC 166)

Dk lavender blue
(DMC 3838)

Very dk
blue violet
(DMC 333)

Chartreuse
(DMC 703)

Br green
(DMC 700)

Alphabet 1: Floral Monogram

Copy at 400%

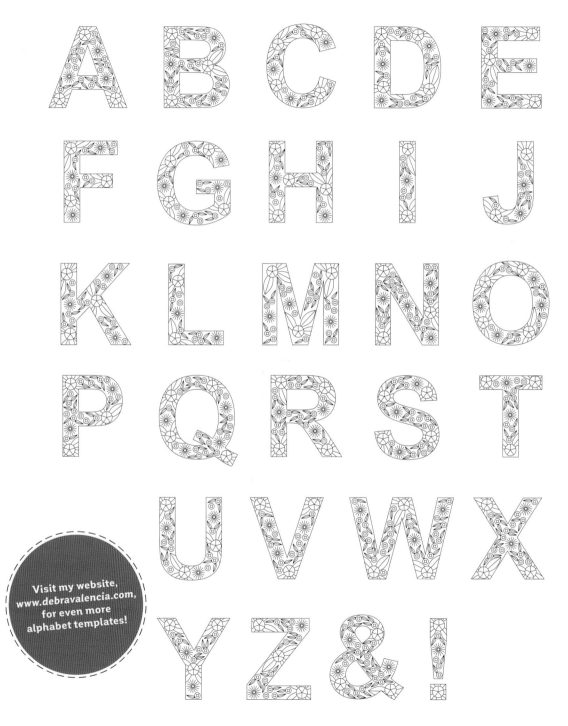

Visit my website, www.debravalencia.com, for even more alphabet templates!

Alphabet 2: Welcome Sign Name Drop

Copy at 150%

Alphabet 3: Monogram Gift Tag

Copy at 400%

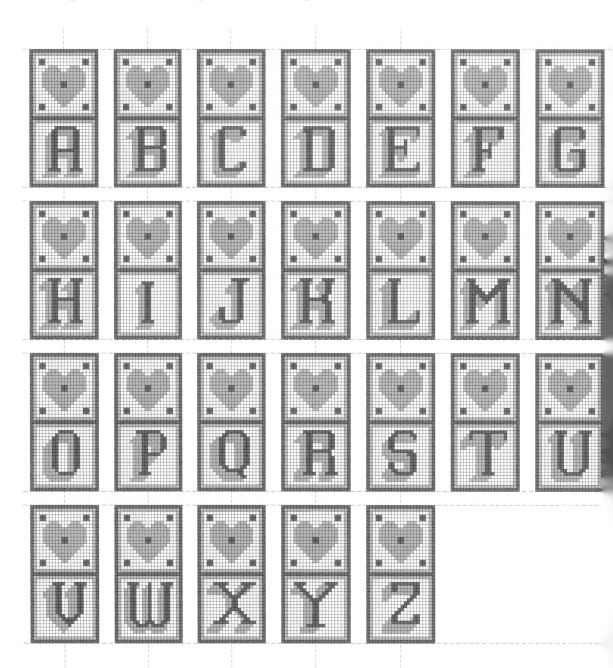

Alphabet 4: Name Tag

Copy at 100%

Alphabet 5: Tennis Shoe Monogram | Left Foot

Copy at 400%

Alphabet 5: Tennis Shoe Monogram | Right Foot

Copy at 400%

Alphabet 6: Luggage Tag

Copy at 150%

Alphabet 7: Bonus

Copy at 400%

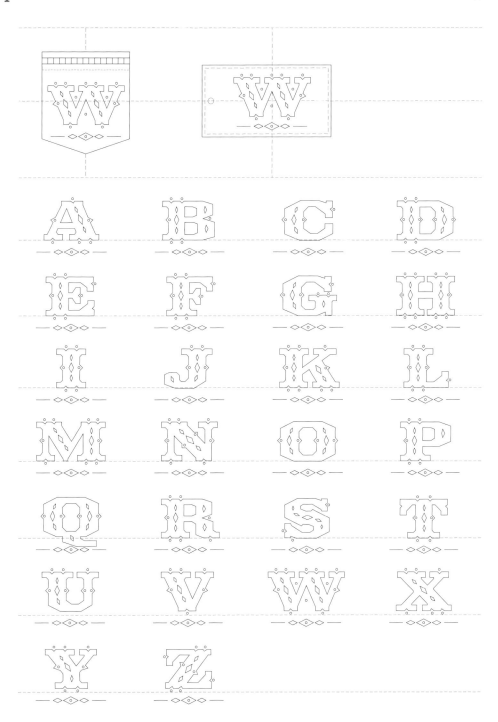

Index

accessories
  Airport Code Luggage Tags, *150–53 (172)*
  Bookworm Fabric Bookmarks, *126–29*
  Four Eyed and Fabulous Eyeglass Case, *118–21*
  Get Organized Canvas Pouches, *140–43*
  Hello Gorgeous Cosmetic Bag, *122–25*
  Monogram Cross-Stitch Gift Tags, *130–33 (168)*
  Personalizing Name Labels (or Everything), *144–49 (169)*
  Reduce, Recycle, Reuse Tote Bag, *134–39*
alphabets, 166–73

backstitch, 24
bags. *See* accessories
blanket stitch, 25

canvas, waste, 15–16
circular straight stitch, 53
clothing and shoes. *See also* accessories
  Geometric Monogram Tennis Shoes, *154–57 (170–171)*
  Summer of Love Jeans Pocket, *162–65*
  Wild and Free Shirt, *158–61*
colonial knot stitch, 26–27
colors of thread, 14
couching (trellis) stitch, 27–29
cross-stitch, 30–31

design transfer methods, 17–18
double herringbone stitch, 38

embroidery scissors, 12–13

fabric-covered hoop back, 21
fabrics
  interfacing, 15
  prewashing, 15
  ready-made items, 16
  thread count, 15
  waste canvas, 15–16
finishing projects, 19
fishbone stitch, 31–32
frames. *See* hoops and frames
French knot, 34–35

gathered hoop back, 20–21
glove stitch, 36

herringbone stitches, 37, 38
home décor
  Always Kiss Me Pillowcase Set, *100–103*
  Classic Cocktail Coasters, *90–93*
  Days of the Week Tea Towels, *94–99*
  Magic Lumbar Accent Pillow, *104–7*
  "Stop" Brick Doorstop, *108–13*
  Top to Bottom Bath Towel, *114–17*
hoops and frames
  about: displaying/mounting embroideries in, 20–21; fabric-covered back, 21; gathered back, 20–21; glue gun for mounting pieces in, 20; types and choosing, 13
  Commemorative Motherhood Frame, *86–89*
  Floral Monogram Hoop, *62–65 (166)*
  International Symbol of Welcome, *82–85 (167)*
  Life Is Too Short to Drink Cheap Champagne Oval Hoop, *74–77*
  Me Casa es Su Casa Hoop, *66–69*
  My Happy Place Frame, *78–81*
  Question Mark Art Hoop, *70–73*
  Watercolor Rainbow Hoop, *58–61*

interfacing, 15

labels and tags. *See* accessories
lazy daisy stitch, 39
light table and pen, for transferring templates, 17–18
long and short stitch, 39–41

magnifier, 13

needles, 12

pen and light table, for transferring templates, 17–18
pillows. *See* home décor
prewashing fabrics, 15
projects. *See also* accessories; clothing and shoes; home décor; hoops and frames
  design transfer methods, 17–18
  finishing, 19
  materials for, 15–16
  overview of, 8
  ready-made items for, 16
  thread colors and, 14
  tools for, 12–13

random straight stitch, 54
ribbon rose stitch, 41–42
rosette stitch, 43–44
running stitches, 45, 46

satin stitch, 47
scissors, 12–13
seed stitch, 48
sheaf stitch, 49–50
star stitch, 50–51
stem stitch, 52
stitches
  backstitch, 24
  blanket stitch, 25
  colonial knot, 26–27
  couching (trellis) stitch, 27–29
  cross-stitch, 30–31
  double herringbone stitch, 38
  fishbone stitch, 31–32
  fly stitch, 33–34
  French knot, 34–35
  glove stitch, 36
  herringbone stitches, 37, 38
  lazy daisy stitch, 39
  long and short stitch, 39–41
  ribbon rose stitch, 41–42
  rosette stitch, 43–44
  running stitches, 45, 46
  satin stitch, 47
  seed stitch, 48
  sheaf stitch, 49–50
  star stitch, 50–51
  stem stitch, 52
  straight stitch (circular), 53
  straight stitch (random), 54
  waste knot, 55
  whipped running stitch, 46
straight stitch (circular), 53
straight stitch (random), 54
Sulky Sticky Fabri-Solvy, 17

templates, transferring, 17–18
Tennis shoes, geometric monogram, *154–57 (170–171)*
text/alphabets, 166–73
thimbles, 12
thread, colors of, 14
thread count, 15
tools, 12–13
transfer paper, 18
transferring designs, 17–18
trellis (couching) stitch, 27–29
triadic colors, 14

washing embroideries, 19
washing fabrics before embroidering, 15
waste canvas, 15–16
waste knot, 55
whipped running stitch, 46

About the Author

Debra Valencia, a visionary artist, designer, and entrepreneur with a passion for world travel, artisan traditions, pop art, fashion, and everything vintage, has branded a modern look uniquely her own. Her designs take a fresh approach to creatively blending floral, paisley, geometric, and decorative motifs with a distinctive sense of style. Her bright colors and bold elements can be described as chic and sassy. Debra's artwork is licensed to dozens of manufacturers in the gift, stationery, textiles, home décor, fashion accessories, and beauty industries, with thousands of products in a variety of retailers.

Debra graduated with honors with a BFA from the University of the Arts in Philadelphia. She worked as a graphic designer and creative director for several companies in the early years of her career. She has won numerous professional design awards, such as AIGA's 50 Best Books of the Year. Her work has been featured in dozens of publications, including *Time*, *Communication Arts*, *Print*, *Abitare*, *Elle Décor*, *Greetings Etc.*, and *Giftware News*, to name a few.

As art educator, Debra has served as a part-time faculty member at Otis College of Art & Design in Los Angeles for over 15 years and at Art Center College of Design in Pasadena for over five years. Courses taught include Business of Art Licensing, Surface/Textile Design, Graphic Design, Typography, and more. Debra has lectured at major institutions, including Cal Poly Tech, Harvard University, University of Wisconsin, and FIDM, and national conferences such as AIGA (American Institute of Graphic Arts), SEGD (Society of Experiential Graphic Designers), and AFCI (Association for Creative Industries). She has served as a judge of her peers in numerous national design competitions.

Debra is an experienced seamstress and has been enjoying needle arts and other crafts since childhood. Her designs have been produced as quilting fabric collections for Fabric Editions, South Sea Imports, Wilmington Prints, and David Textiles, resulting in thousands

of yards sold since 2009. She is the co-author of *Sewing Pretty Bags* and the author of four designer coloring books, all published under Design Originals.

Debra lives in Los Angeles, CA, in a Cliff May mid-century modern home built in 1953, surrounded by vintage collectibles, iconic furniture by Charles Eames and George Nelson, and original artwork by her artist friends. Debra's son, Westin Walker, is an illustrator, graphic designer, and fine artist with a BFA from California College of Art. He collaborates on professional projects with his mother and contributed the stitching artwork diagrams for this book.

Author Website and Contact

Visit the DIY section of Debra's website, where you will find free patterns and project ideas. Please follow her on Facebook, Instagram, and YouTube for news, updates, and demos. She would love to hear from you and see your creations. Feel free to post questions, comments, and photos to share with other fans on social media.

Links:
www.debravalencia.com/diy
www.facebook.com/debravalenciadesign
www.instagram.com/debravalencia